Praise

C000142559

'*Five Horizons* offers a wealth of insight and knowledge that will prove useful to anyone involved in business, whether a start-up or corporate leader.'

— **Tony Cooper, Chairman**, LegalDW, former partner at Deloitte and Merryck & Co.

'This is a book for now. Contemporary and of the moment, it completely captures the need for entrepreneurs and business leaders to challenge and change the existing unhelpful paradigms. It is a book for people who want to create a business; for those who are challenged by conventional business structures and "we always do it this way" mindsets; for those who struggle with existing risk-aversity; and for those who are unable to get their point across because the whole investment structure is tilted heavily against the best ideas for change. I learned a lot!'

— **Stephen Chadwick**, President EMEA, Hexagon MI

'This is the most compelling argument for driving change in business that I have read, as scripted by one of the most innovative practitioners. This is the type of book that the CEO of an organisation would give to their executive team in an attempt to make them understand, and think, in a more entrepreneurial way.'

— **Joe Bridgeman**, director and advisor

'Polished, pragmatic, positive, *Five Horizons* is thought-provoking and incredibly helpful for entrepreneurs, who will reference it often. The balance of practical suggestions and positivity for our future, along with real-life stories, is a winning formula. As an entrepreneur, I found it helpful to read Steve's pragmatic advice and experiences of what had and hadn't worked in his career. I love that all of this is woven in with the socioeconomics of how we might positively embrace the Great Shift and operate as businesses that our world needs to continue in a healthy way – aligning our universal laws with our hearts and minds, rather than just money or greed.'

— **Lisa Burton, CEO**, LegalDW

FIVE

HORIZONS

HOW TO SUCCEED IN THE AGE
OF STAKEHOLDER CAPITALISM

STEVE SANDERS

First published in 2022 by
Panoma Press Ltd
www.rethinkpress.com
www.panomapress.com

Cover design and book layout by Neil Coe

978-1-78452-974-1

First published in Great Britain in 2022 by Panoma Press
(www.panomapress.com)

This book is dedicated to the numerous open-minded, stoic people who persisted with my best ideas, keeping the faith even though these ideas were disruptive, nonconformist and often difficult to grasp. We mud-wrestled in a hostile environment until we succeeded.

Contents

Introduction

We are entering a time of changes in underlying go-to-market conditions that generally aren't foreseeable, at least not without a considerably altered mindset. The aim of this book is to enlighten and equip you, so that you may secure market leadership and improve company-level value during this time of disruptive transition.

Do you have many stakeholders who depend upon you for the impact of your business? Do you know that predicates even greater future success, but you lack the clarity to execute that? Do you understand the mission criticality of satisfying your implicit duty of care to all – customers and shareholders first, but also employees, suppliers, the environment and communities wherever you make an impact; satisfying government and regulators at home and in all markets; and all this amid a changing profile of investors or lenders? Then this book is for you.

The world is changing

Public opinion, among those generations soon to be aged twenty to fifty, increasingly represents a clear and present threat to business. During the next ten to fifteen years, humanity will fundamentally change in terms of what and how we buy and consume, and why we decide to work for any given company. Our elders and the governments and businesses they operate are responsible for all global societies reaching a precipice of globally catastrophic proportions.

It's likely you'll doubt this because you haven't witnessed it before. Nobody has. We are at a crucial moment in the history of our species, at which it appears we are failing to act judiciously, expeditiously or with respect for the significance of our momentous historical duty. What is more pitiful is that an addiction to consumerism and an insatiable thirst for perpetually growing profit – our basest human urges – seem likely to precipitate our fall.

Human habitual patterns mean that change will not be self-administered, at least not quickly enough for our deadline. Regulatory change of unprecedented scale is the only way to transform us all quickly enough, yet those able to facilitate this change are hampered in that duty. They are bound to an implied obligation to moderate impact on those major businesses whose taxes in turn fuel the system of government that they govern.

Your role in business and why it matters

There is a positive here, and this book poses that positive as a calling for business leaders to provide leadership. If you class yourself as a business leader, now is your time to step up and heed the call of history to make a difference.

Imagine the effect of a small lever flipping railway tracks to divert 30-ton carriages in the direction of safety or peril. We too must examine what small steps can achieve the right outcomes. Not dramatically perhaps, but gradually. When additive effects of small changes are viewed as a whole, history may judge us as having been fit for purpose.

We are not spiritual leaders, nor do we hold significant influence over nations or cultures. We are in business, and that is a good starting point for us to seek ways of solving the demands placed on us in that capacity.

Consumers and employees of 2025–2040 will expect so much more, and those who don't match up to that will fail. Those who take advantage of this moment can create new forms of differentiation that will cause customers and employees to gravitate towards them and offer their loyalty. It is likely that those who choose to wait and see, or their businesses at least, will perish.

Why me?

The challenge I have described is something I feel strangely familiar with. Success will first demand people embrace fundamental changes in their lives – both you as a leader and others. At first you will be an outlier, a nonconformist or contrarian. The mindset of those inside the core normality will resist. You need to navigate that so the tangent proposed is one that can and will be embraced by all.

Throughout the thirty years of my career, I've chosen to be that outlier. Most people tended to reject or lack interest in looking outside norms, or beyond boundaries and mindset, perpetuating systems of work in which they comfortably existed. My role has been to challenge people, teams, companies, business ecosystems and their markets to change, either forcefully through pivotal direction shifts or by gently course-correcting.

I have learned that even when the new ways are necessary for survival, resistance is so forceful that one can be repelled as though an enemy. This situation remains until the discomfort of change is less than the pain of remaining the same. In normal circumstances, time is our friend, and we wait patiently for laggards to catch up. In these pressing circumstances when fickle customers and employees will turn away once better, more sustainable alternatives emerge, I cannot see a relaxed attitude to lapsed time as being anything but our enemy.

There is an art, skill set, mindset and toolkit that enables me to turn that intransigence and inertia into forward momentum. These tools and attributes can also help you to achieve great things, but, for our greater purpose, there isn't enough time to share that face to face.

In this book I aim to help you to be one of those who survive and thrive, and, in doing so, to improve the level of stakeholder impact we achieve collectively around the world. You must decide that this 'tough news' isn't just a figment of Steve's imagination but a lucky early warning of things to come. You will work to leverage foresight and achieve advantages in business. Your ego security and leadership will not be fragile, so you will be able to reveal vulnerabilities and collaborate to cross boundaries and reinvent.

How to use this book

Don't be distracted by my storytelling or the trails of breadcrumbs I've included here. That is my conscious choice. I don't believe people absorb new insights better because they are provided in tidy lists. I choose to blend styles, to encourage you to enjoy absorbing knowledge you will retain and recall when needed.

It will be the stories that leave a lasting impression, not lists of detail. Remember that you too communicate better that way. Although you may try regurgitating lists of facts, eventually you will revert. Before mass media, when we fell into the trap of imagining that humans absorb ideas recited from textbooks and process maps, people used stories to pass on experience – as I do, and as you do, too. To help those who need it, at the end of this introduction I provide a clear overall context for each chapter and signposts to what you'll gain, which will make it easy to locate specific content.

I don't intend this book to be an exposé revealing uncomfortable secrets from real cases. That would be unfair and could embarrass real people or damage the reputation of companies or government departments. I occasionally switch into purely fictional storytelling that conveys the essence of lessons learned, drawing on multiple experiences to create stories in my imagination. Any similarity to real-life situations is purely coincidental.

Chapter 1 describes a 'Great Shift' in market dynamics, perhaps unseen and immeasurable, yet taking shape as a critical change in ways of thinking across societies. Its impact amounts to an unparalleled threat and opportunity. Such disruptions, not recessions, cause sector-specific company extinctions. This Great Shift will swiftly affect many sectors in different ways and soon will affect you.

Chapter 2 addresses the question of why people have not reacted with activism to threats that are perceived as being out of sight, out of mind despite their seriousness. You will discover why and how people respond differently as threats take on urgency based on rapidly changing proximity to those they care about more.

Chapter 3 helps you to grasp the presence of tipping points in moving market dynamics, without needing precise data to accept this as being true. Lift the curtain and peek outside your present viewpoint or comfort zone, and you'll see a mass of conscious yet unfulfilled desires that await a new alternative to satisfy them; perhaps from you, or else from a competitor.

Chapter 4 describes how business is the most agile, powerful vehicle to achieve change. There is no singular central source of leadership or genius that will solve all issues. Compulsion to change comes from the masses, ignited when business offers new alternatives, and pressure is applied to regulators and governments to accelerate towards a better new norm.

Chapter 5 asks you to reconsider the inevitability of pure shareholder primacy, and acknowledge a shifting priority from that paradigm. It explains the origins and history of companies in their current form and traces our journey through profit obsession and forgiveness of all wrongdoing, to the point today where the Great Shift will drive us all to reconfigure to achieve purpose-led modes of doing business.

Chapter 6 helps you to escape conditioned thinking and assumed norms by finding ways of allowing nonconformists and contrarians into your strategic planning process and using structured planning models that help capture value from their insights to build a better version of you and your business for the future.

Chapters 7 and 8 confront the fact that you may need to behave in a way that is contrary to your instincts if you are to get the best from all those around you. They suggest techniques to help you get the best from collaborating in strategic engagement across ecosystems – inspiring others as champions and joining up to decide how to position yourself – based on principles and value drivers defined as being meaningful.

Chapters 9 and 10 help to translate these ideas into systematic value delivery. Exploring culture and the use of frameworks to challenge yourself and others, you will cyclically improve the various aspects of strategy. Going into more detail about the use of tools, disciplines and best practices, these chapters show the various interlocks between company-level strategy and how you work on business readiness, major deals, client plans and the product or service go-to-market.

Chapters 11 and 12 challenge you to embrace the true power of purpose and show you how to articulate how and why your business can differentiate. They provide evidence that it is inevitable that a purpose-led strategy will become the most critical factor in remaining competitive and attractive to customers and employees during the coming years.

The answer must be to align everything that you do, that you consume or produce with the things that people care about most deeply at a human level, and to solve issues you can address as widely as possible in ecosystems you affect. At this moment in history, getting this right could be the most important thing you've done.

1

Behold, The Great Shift

Things change precisely when you least expect it. Even the biggest changes. Even mass extinction events. Consider the fate of the fearless dodo, sitting atop the food chain in sixteenth-century Mauritius. One day humans landed, the dodo became lunch, and later, extinct. Ask yourself, 'What would the dodo do, if only the dodo knew?', and then ask yourself, 'What should I do now?'

Once I've explained the idea of the Great Shift, the next step is to convince you it's a real thing. Ironic really. We will demand absolute evidence of the biggest threat to mass business extinction, yet readily accept and mitigate threats of less impact. Yes, you guessed it, the greater threat is more costly to you too. Not convinced?

Choice not to act upon disruptive shifts is behind peaks in company failures. One such peak, across many markets, will result from many factors stemming from a generational transition. This will be transformational as we accelerate towards a precipice beyond which the fabric of markets must be irreversibly changed. You need to accept that businesspeople will be instruments of this

Great Shift and decide to participate. By your inaction you could be perceived as part of the problem.

There is a critical change occurring in our way of thinking as a species that will manifest across societies worldwide. All of us will feel the effects of this, as it impacts buying decisions, employment choices and the basis on which companies compete in their markets. Ultimately, such a Great Shift will trigger pan-sector business extinction events for those that don't prepare.

Recessions don't kill businesses; disruptions do

Over 140 years and across sectors, there has been little correlation between recessions and high levels of company failures. Peaks of failures arise from the inability or unwillingness to adapt to disruptive discontinuities, and changes affecting the underpinnings of a market, its cost base and competitive dynamics. Clayton Christensen's theory of disruptive innovation, first published in the 1990s, is far from indisputably correct in all interpretations, but it works as a useful frame of reference for this purpose.[1]

Understanding this theory was a key moment for me at Warwick Business School (WBS). I was reading proof that my suspicions were correct, which gave me new evidence in my argument that we should care more about innovations and the threat posed to established businesses.[2]

I realised that not all ideas classed as 'disruptive innovations' are born equal, and that we need to test, challenge and prove the claims of ego-led innovators.

---

1   Christensen, *The Innovator's Dilemma*
2   Warwick Business School, www.wbs.ac.uk

I began to ask whether each disruptive idea had any realistic chance of affecting the markets' dynamics, enough to cause a real competitive discontinuity, and whether those not acting upon it would consequently lose attractiveness and suffer lost demand.

Sector-specific discontinuities cause sector-specific extinction events – self-inflicted culling for those with the least foresight. This will be a pan-sector extinction event affecting businesses globally and across sectors.

Some rare examples affect many sectors at once. The most familiar shifts are caused by application of technologies. New business models sit behind the scenes but are equally impactful. Less considered are the shifts that stem from culture, across societies and even humanity overall. Any of these can result in the emergence of pan-sector extinction events affecting businesses globally, and these are central to the message of this book.

Obvious examples are technological – the rapid changes in glass production technology being an interesting sector-specific trigger that was repeated through multiple, equally disruptive, sector-specific discontinuities in the early twentieth century.

More familiar is the Internet, which we think of as the 'uber-disruptor'. In fact, the discontinuity effect is experienced over time, sector by sector. Trigger points only occur when forces play out in each sector that create the kind of competitive impact I described above.

The Internet of Things (IoT) is said to be one such universal disruptor, capturing streams of data from every imaginable device, yet this is evidence that a technology needs a business model before it can truly cause discontinuity. You'd never claim rubber tyres were the innovation that led to the automotive revolution. Such sweeping claims would ignore the need for so many more layers of innovation.

The IoT is only now beginning to affect insurance. First, new Artificial Intelligence (AI) was needed, able to interpret IoT data, to predict and prevent risks. Insurers then built and price differentiated new property insurance products. Peers in global property insurance markets are observing the work of a small UK insurer who has been first to market with this, and they must react quickly as that first mover has a differentiated lead.

A new one for many of you will be the predictions that there will be a plant-based protein disruption somewhere between 2020 and 2040. Expert modelling from the US predicts up to 40% of the market will move to being plant-based even without regulatory changes. By that time, alternative dairy will account for 60% of the market share. While many other pieces of the puzzle need to be aligned, I'd say that's something that burger companies, cheese producers and farmers need to take seriously.[3]

Business model shifts have surfaced in the 'as-a-service' and 'pay-per-use' phenomena that are seemingly everywhere, from e-bikes propped on every corner to unlikely bespoke dog food services designed to meet doggy's personal needs and supplied monthly to the door.

---

3   Dongoski, 'Plant-based protein predictions'

Not long ago those of us championing these shifts faced disbelief, and even ridicule from many quarters. Imagine other shifts, perhaps even great shifts, that you might disbelieve when revealed to you.

Those who vote 'non'

There are sectors that firmly hold onto their legacy paradigms, with executives who resist unreasonably. Perhaps they intend to continue simply building and selling products while a service-led paradigm is emerging. Consumers no longer want their products, nor do they benefit from them.

I'd like to share a story with you, and yes, it might seem familiar to you but that's only because it is an amalgam of multiple businesses I've engaged with. This multinational is heading for a digitally enabled pay-per-use future. The response in many countries: a sadly predictable 'wait and see' or 'we'll think about it'.

This could be any business locked in a mentality that their traditional physical product is the limit of value customers can derive from them. Let's say, for argument's sake, motor cars are the physical product, and digital access to varying modes of mobility on demand is their digitally enabled future. The same could be said of hotels fixated on selling room space when their future is shifting to make most profit from cross-selling guests various experiences to augment the hotel visit.

The reason for reluctance to accept shifts like those is that it seems to be an exaggerated risk. Any suggestion that invisible society-wide cultural change will soon cause such a grave discontinuity seems absurd from within the core mindset. Only once the competitive alternative is offered to customers will they reveal the true extent of their desire for that alternative.

You might similarly resist my prescience of a Great Shift, preferring to focus narrowly on technology-based advancements as the only relevant competitive consideration. You will read later that in such a mindset you could suffer from a delusion that you can and should be able to predict how your world will turn. In our reality, the innumerable variables of the global human organism will affect your market in ways that are frankly unforeseeable, especially to conformist minds conditioned to the current paradigm.

Consider where we've seen many such shifts being embraced and capitalised upon in markets. Look at pervading attitudes to antiracism, antisexism and openness to gender fluidity, and how this affected entertainment, fashion and retail sectors. This has now caused a complete overhaul of the way the media makes funding decisions, and a refresh of historical libraries of entertainment and advertisement content. The sole aim is to satisfy rapidly changing views of acceptability. Many would say that is a good thing, an opportunity to rid ourselves of cringeworthy 1970s negative stereotypes.

In 2010 did you foresee the severity of that global cultural shift and its impact?

New media production projects, competing for funds, are being evaluated for inclusiveness of these topics. The October 2021 British Film Institute film expo schedule was clear evidence of these cultural shifts. Arguably, any brand failing to consider such clear evidence of pan-sector shifts will face a difficult future.

Generational change

For products and services, at every stage of the supply chain, and in every part of the value chain, decisions are made by people.

Attitude changes in populations reach a relevant critical mass as generations age and their spending- and employee-power increases. In hindsight, after each major generation change, we see massive shifts in attitudes that have driven demand and employment transformations.

Smart businesspeople need to think about this in advance. I aim to bring you closer to the pulse of that shift – by looking back to history, then at the present and then considering the future.

Respice, adspice, prospice: examine the past before examining the present, and then examine the future.

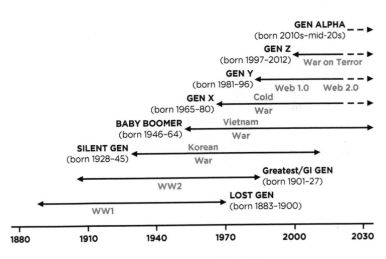

Generations – birth years and work life span

This discourse about the theory of generations relates more precisely to the timeline and experiences in Western countries.

There will be parallel experiences in other societies that we can draw from, which will reflect similarities, albeit according to the economic and social patterns that have developed there.[4]

In twentieth-century developed or industrialised nations, an illusion was perpetuated of an employer–employee bond they called 'job for life'. This mantra for pre-war parents and the baby boomer generation (born after 1945 and before the mid-1960s) temporarily held employers, employees and their children to an unsustainable expectation.

Though only lasting perhaps forty years post war, it affected how people made employment and buying decisions. My parents' generation were conflicted. They celebrated collectivism, with which their parents had survived during and after the war. In a tug of war, this higher calling competed with the baby boomers' own special form of aspirational selfishness.

Proud middle- and working-class baby boomers felt compelled to reward people and companies by that double standard. The winners needed to reflect those impossibly high collectivism standards, yet also had to satisfy a generation's burgeoning greed: desiring to stabilise their own futures and to acquire material quality and quantity.

Fend for yourselves, that's the way.

---

4   Mannheim, 'The problem of generations', described in National Academies of Sciences, Engineering, and Medicine, *Are Generational Categories Meaningful Distinctions for Workforce Management?*

Unsurprisingly, Generation X (born between 1965 and 1980) were first to feel the end of that unsustainable paradigm. They grew up amid economic hardship and recoveries of the 1970s and early 1980s, and then entered the workplace.

Admittedly, I recall these experiences as a member of Generation X who was also challenged with attempting social mobility. I was from an inner-city, low socioeconomic background and my relatives had little or no educational or professional advice to offer me. My own family's circumstances may have been untypical to many in Britain. I believe, however, that my experience of attempting social mobility in the 1980s was similar to that of many others at different times and in different cultures around the world.

Other nations in all continents reflected this to a greater or lesser extent during times of hardship and transformation. Not least of these were those in Eastern Europe and Russia, who experienced it in a hurried way after the end of the Soviet Union in the 1990s. No one culture can claim this discomfort uniquely.

My first memories at work were hearing, 'We won't give you a job for life, but we will equip you to be employable.' Company guaranteed pension schemes closed only months prior to my entry into employment. Trade unions were castrated and toothless, so talk of collective bargaining for employees was muted. I found myself thrust, ill-prepared, into an emerging reality of 'fend for yourselves'.

There we stood on a personal precipice, feeling pressure to earn more, more quickly. We responded by changing jobs to climb the ladder, resulting in criticism from our elders. Baby boomer seniors disapproved of our impatience over pushing forward new ideas and our desire for progress that stretched their perception of acceptability.

Gen X are remembered as being guilty of short-termism, greed and selfishness. Looking back, I beg to differ. Consider how, in the 1980s and 1990s, these young adults reacted according to their circumstances. Maturing, they were being told by comfortable, well-provided-for elders that they would not be able to provide for the basic future security of their children's generation. In Maslow's Hierarchy of Needs, Gen X's shelter and sustenance were at stake.[5] Gen X knew they would receive little help and would have to rely on their own efforts and ingenuity. They proceeded to do precisely what they'd been told to do – fend for themselves. Employment and buying choices disregarded pretences of collectivism.

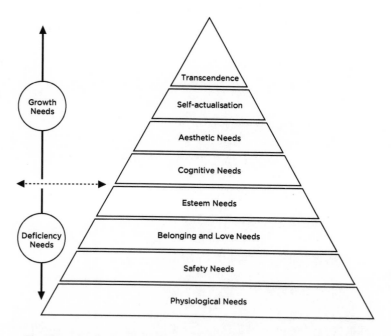

The Hierarchy of Human Needs, adapted from Maslow's Hierarchy of Needs

---

5   Maslow, 'A theory of human motivation'

This is nothing new. Look back at generations in the late nineteenth and early twentieth centuries. Their revolution was one of challenging male-dominated, conservative, command-and-control culture at work, in politics and family life. Aristocracy and traditional families clung to status and power, resisting change, even though this was dangerously irrelevant and burdensome. By the 1930s, music, dance, fashion, politics, employment and family had all shifted. Opinions considered disruptive and antisocial in 1895 had been normalised by 1935.

This is the way of humanity. Ideally, we should listen to new generations and adapt. Slowly, or perhaps quickly, if need be, but change we must. Resistance will often lead to revolution but change itself, as you will soon realise, is inevitable. We've seen it in art, workers' rights, contraception, interracial marriages and almost all parts of life, yet today, somehow – either through innocence, self-superiority or stupidity – there's resistance to accepting a Great Shift could happen now.

While you see evidence of great shifts littered throughout history, you too might perceive we are so advanced that somehow there's no space for it today. You wouldn't be the first to be so badly mistaken.

Our youngest generations have inherited a machine that has built-in resistance to change and cannot change by itself. They've inherited a world that has no time left to bargain with. This realisation unequivocally unites them *all*, globally. The reality in today's integrated, overindebted and consumerist-focused world is that the machine cannot cope with the change that we need it to self-impose.

The machine is addicted to growth. Millennials and
Gen Z are beginning to realise there's no hope in
asking a sick man to amputate his own leg.
We can't trust the machine to change by itself.

Technically, our world is unsustainably addicted to unhealthy growth, with a debt-based model underpinning global economy. Banks relentlessly exchange vast quantities of new virtual debt, often without the backing of a lasting asset such as gold. Responding to this value vacuum, they print increasingly vast quantities of new currency. That currency needs to be circulated, spent on products or invested in more and more projects. Inflation and currency devaluation are inevitable and will be increasingly severe due to the out-of-control upward spiral of new currency.

The only answer is to slow down, but the machine won't do that. It cannot do that because it's addicted to growth. Demand growth is our oxygen, but it increases attraction to a destructive black hole with maximum gravitational pull. The global economy seems to be spiralling into it without a remedy or rescue plan – except perhaps a vain hope that by going faster we could miraculously spin out on the far side.

Millennials and Generation Z know what is needed. They need to stop the madness. Those with early clarity, admittedly not quite yet the majority, are telling us all that we need to slow down and buy more modestly. They are imploring those who produce to do so more sensibly.

To achieve that, some profit needs to be sacrificed in exchange for sustainability. This generation demands it constantly, yet what they witness is that the machine is incapable of changing.

Reluctantly and resentfully, younger generations perpetuate the status quo, but not for long. An older generation is in charge but is not in control, and it is, for the time being, either unable to change or unwilling to.

That is the catch-22 of Millennials and Gen Z. Generations that by virtue of external factors are motivated by global collectivism, perhaps more than any generation before them. Generations that realise those who tell us they're in charge are not really in control. Generations being told to simply, 'Trust the untrustable machine.'

What then do you imagine will be their next step? When will they take that step? We know in business 'we are the sicknesses' – when will the antibodies attack?

Developed industrialised nations have formed a way of life supported by generally accepted assumptions about existence. This is aggressively reinforced by entertainment, politics and media. Collectively, it tells us that we have got it all correct. Our empires will endure. Keep calm and carry on.

Wealthy middle-class minorities account for most consumerist demand. They see themselves at the top of the economic food chain, but this picture is changing, and their dominance is weakening. They are being replaced by billions in supply-side countries around the world, consumers who are aging, educating and accumulating wealth. Those long-suffering 'developing nations' are emerging as new demand hubs and have a hand on the tiller of production capacity, having until now taken the brunt of mistreatment in the old world order.

These emerging ecosystem power hubs will inevitably seek to improve the circumstances in their societies and will become more judicious over how they deploy supply-side capacity.

Sociological changes will both affect the supply-side capacity and create unforeseen demand patterns and sources of innovation. Generational attitudes will affect counterparts in developed nations, speeding us towards a tipping point moment.

The end of glorious empires

With diminishing power atop the economic food chain, it's becoming clear we are not the shining knights in this story. The system that we've created has formed an abscess on the global human organism, potentially a malignant cancer. There is no time to slowly heal holistically, nor even to self-medicate. We can only hope that antibodies will flood in and try to correct this imbalance and disharmony.

Historically, the end of empires has been signalled by internal conflict, social disorder and moral corruption, overspending, unwise military and public spending, and a chaotic collapse of currencies and industry. Leadership loses credibility and fails under the weight of its own inadequacy, as the scale of complexity is not controllable by those who pretend to be in control. You may have seen signs of this, perhaps in the situations in developed nations you are familiar with.

Most empires didn't just disappear. They evolved into tourist sites, monuments of past greatness and sources of lessons that we still fail to heed. Today, the simple tasks of operating industry, stable governance and social cohesion have become illusive at best. Their 'old way' was considered either irrelevant or toxic to the greater good, and their dominance died.

No, I don't claim that the next Great Shift will amount to one empire being wiped out and replaced by another. Our world today is a multitude of empires, distinct, connected through alliances, interlocked and interdependent, in social and economic webs. These webs will possibly outlive any twenty-first-century event; for instance, were one superpower, at worst, to lose 10% to another.

The global human organism's antibodies will be the instrument of this Great Shift. Those antibodies will flow organically, and business will feel the effect quickest. Changing attitudes and values will affect buying, supply and employment choices in our newest generations who, within a few years, will account for most of our workers and customers. These generations will act synchronously and globally. Business will be the first to experience the effects of that Great Shift, and they will be a barometer of what will soon affect whole economies and societies.

People are globally and unconsciously causing the shift.

The global movement I hypothesise is made up of people who are influenced across country boundaries, who are being more selective in choosing who to work for. They are directing consumption demand on a different basis and make decisions based on life experience – decisions about which companies to support when buying products or when supplying their newly innovative production capabilities.

The global human organism needs to fix itself and be flooded with antibodies to suffocate the sickness. Choices among businesses, to adapt or not to, will determine which will survive.

This entire generation of people feed into a global supply chain and consumption market. In the 2020 pandemic they demonstrated they can go lean, do without, slow down production and consumption, stop buying or buy an alternative. It is quite realistic to expect they will opt to do whatever it takes to kill the sickness.

You might not see it happening if you're focused on what's under your nose. Like driving on a highway, you only see the cars ahead and behind, and your focus might be on the race to pass them and reach your destination sooner. Only by rising above, taking a global view, do you see the truth that nobody is getting anywhere quicker, and that only by slowing down together will we all collectively go faster.

Take a deep breath and pause to let this soak in. The world as you know it is, to all practical purposes, gone and changed forever. The effects might only just be reaching you now, or maybe they haven't yet. They will do soon.

The burgeoning demand globally, from Millennials and Gen Z, is asking for better from the machine, but the better alternative has not yet been provided. There is a desire for holistically sustainable, democratic, socially conscious business, with a lot more 'eco' and inclusiveness, and a little less 'ego' and selfishness. The expectation is for a lot more creating and a little less taking. A burgeoning demand is waiting in abeyance until a good alternative becomes available.

In summary, you need to be alert to the Great Shift that is approaching an unforeseen tipping point, and even more so because it's not obvious to onlookers. This is crucial because it is a source of discontinuity affecting market dynamics and likely to cause an extinction event affecting those who don't heed warnings. You've read evidence of this in lesser shifts, and a hypothesis of how this shift could amplify the effects of disruption across multiple markets at once.

We are going through a unique convergence of generational shift with the presence of external drivers that are compelling us all to change how we compete for the attention of customers and employees. The scale of that threat to your business should not be underestimated nor ignored.

A reality is dawning upon the masses, who are now firm in their view that many of our existential global issues arose because of consumer ignorance, perpetuated and manipulated by business practices of those driven primarily by greed, and worsened by what is perceived as ambivalence or incompetency of government.

The Great Shift is upon us. This is universal. It is absolute.

2

Even Remote Threats Become Personal

In the previous chapter, I described a rapidly approaching, multifaceted Great Shift that is precipitating unexpectedly and suddenly, a Great Shift in all markets, each experiencing its effects differently.

As I'm asking you to believe in such a thing as a Great Shift with global potential to affect many or perhaps all sectors of business, I must address a common objection. Based on our collective experience so far, it's fair to doubt the possibility of such cohesive movement across all cultures. One constant seems to be that people don't respond together unless a threat is immediate and affects those who they care about. In this chapter, I will explain the hypothesis behind my belief that this will change.

An existential precipice

It's evident that we're facing a precipice, not just environmentally but in financial markets, public health, climate, international security and many other spheres of life.

If I were to write about these in detail, I'd waste your time and mine. If you don't see this as a truism, I suggest that you do more reading with an open mind. This discourse expects you to accept the reality that our opportunities to step back from the brink are diminishing.

With so many aspects of life likely to topple over respective precipices, there is every reason to anticipate that many of the conditions we consider constants in our world will no longer exist afterwards.

It is also self-evident that this is highest on the agenda for those most immediately threatened, or those most likely to live until the pain becomes real.

A friend recently described what he saw as the self-righteous outcries of Millennials and Gen Z, accusing them of being fickle and feckless in rebellious activism, demanding sustainability or objecting to malfeasance. I disagreed. I can only assume that to convince this baby boomer of the sincerity and worthiness of their conscientious objection there should have been burning of effigies and permanent relocation into hippy villages.

Rebellion may be veiled, but it will be revealed when conditions are right. It could be that rebellion will be unleashed by sheer force of demand, by availability of suitable alternatives that will enjoy a flood of demand, or due to force of regulatory change from central authorities. In time, you will see that all three of those forces tend to act in harmony, one pressing the others forward and all three moving as one. Later, I will write more about this 'virtuous triangle' of three forces.

I will demonstrate my position using an example. I lived in Johannesburg through three years of 1980s apartheid. I felt grievously opposed to those policies, yet, despite this, I admit that I did not take to the streets alongside demonstrators, or face rubber bullets to force a change.

Did that mean my opinion, and the opinions of millions of privately disenchanted South Africans, did not eventually make a difference? Of course, it meant nothing of the sort. The views of millions emerged as a generational shift that made a huge impact. We now know this led to a society-wide change in the 1990s that had been inconceivable only a few years before. To all watching, it was invisible, and they may have suspected the masses were disinterested, until South Africa chose to accept change and later to embrace it.

Let's now look to the general underlying discontent with Russia after its annexation of Crimea and its military practices in the Middle East. That mood was simmering in the psyche of our global community for many years. Observers might have assumed there would be an indefinite state of ambivalence. Perhaps this even emboldened Russian authorities to move on Ukraine more assertively. It was at that moment that, somehow, universally, the mood changed. Seemingly overnight, most countries and most humans decided that extreme punitive measures would be justified, even where they would be harmful to their own lifestyles.

Defending 'my people'

Humans react to fear and danger more urgently than they do to opportunity. That is why the pain of 1980s economic sanctions against apartheid in South Africa had an impact on those who did not willingly choose to change. The journey for refugees to London from Kyiv, Ukraine, is 2,500 km (1,560 miles), whereas from Damascus, Syria, it is 4,500 km (2,800 miles). That 1,700 km difference alone is not enough to account for the significant difference in our global response to Russia in these two situations. In both instances, the level of importance people place based on urgency has something to do with the proximity of threat to their immediate circle. At some point, the potential pain that could be inflicted on their closest community by remaining the same or taking no action exceeded their fear of change. Only then did the mainstream accept that change was needed and action was desirable.

Urgency increases when the potential pain for one's closest community due to remaining the same exceeds the fear of change.

Let's accept that for argument's sake this is hardwired into our instincts from millennia of evolution as social creatures. What is relevant is that this effect increases or decreases conversely to the distance of a threat from our social centre.

Various analogies exist to demonstrate this. While I hesitate to, I will refer to the military one. Please reflect on parallels that should be obvious to you, maybe in sport, business, villages and towns, families and communities. I will touch on these too, of course.[6]

---

6   Travers and Milgram, 'An experimental study of the small world problem'

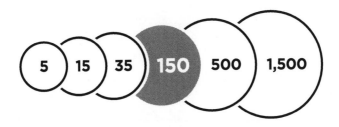

Dunbar's number – the maximum number
of relationships a person can maintain

Dunbar's Number states that we will form up to 150 meaningful relationships, of which thirty-five will be friends, fifteen good friends and five your loved ones. It goes on to describe that our circle can reach 500 acquaintances and 1,500 people we might recognise.

In modern parlance, I've heard it described like this. You might have fifteen people you would perhaps confide in, and up to thirty-five less close friends. You might invite 150 to a gathering. You can recall how you met (on Facebook perhaps) up to 500. The 1,500 (maybe on LinkedIn or Twitter) are people who you might (or might not) recognise by face in the street.

The historical notion of a village tribe sits at around the 150 level. What I have characterised differently is my 'personal universe', comprised of individuals from all three groups. That universe was conceived to describe a changeable subset of around thirty-five people on whom one may depend at various times in life to keep the world moving.

Unit	Approximate no. of people	Consisting of	Commander
Army	100,000	2+ Corps and HQ	General
Corps	30,000+	2+ Divisions	Lt General
Division	15,000+	3 Brigades, HQ, +	Maj General
Brigade	4,500+	3 Regiments, HQ	Brig General
Regiment	1,500+	2+ Battalions, HQ	Colonel
Battalion	700	4+ Companies, HQ	Lt Colonel
Company	175	4 Platoons, HQ	Captain
Platoon	40	4 Squads	Lieutenant
Squad	10		Staff Sergeant

Unit sizes in the US Army[7]

In military life, we can see in real terms how humans interrelate when it concerns life and death, making it a great analogy for this purpose.

The British SAS moves in patrols of four people, the same as a small family unit. Autonomous and isolated, they grow completely dependent on each other for survival. In the case of the SAS these patrols are clustered into troops of sixteen members, much like an extended family. A platoon, in normal military circles the smallest group, numbers thirty to fifty as per our close cohort of friends. After months of mind-numbing training and years of combat, this is where you can observe comrades sacrificing life and limb, acting from instinct to save their cohort from harm.

The company of 80 to 250, like a tribe, needs a command-and-control structure to limit internal competition between platoons.

---

7   MIRECC, 'Unit size (US Army in the late 20th century)'

It is easy to imagine why this is needed to ensure disconnected teams mitigate threats to distant platoons in a theatre of war.

Regiments and battalions are for the mass movement of people and equipment. It's useful to consider older historical choices in the UK to form and name such wide-ranging groups after the region of a country where the troops were recruited; for example, Lancashire, Queen's Cameron Highlanders, or Somerset and Devonshire. Troops were more likely to support orders to face danger knowing that their counterparts ten miles away in France were boys from a neighbouring town. I explain this to emphasise that people react or comply more instinctively in situations where threats affect those they care about.

Conversely, there is sometimes rancour between members of the army and the navy or air force. Worse still is lack of trust between military and civilian personnel. We can imagine how difficult it is to depend upon the human instinct of self-sacrifice between such oversized groups of thousands, living under completely different banners. In NATO or UN peacekeeping corps, considerable technology and operational innovation has been required between allies on the same side, with the simple aim of sharing information that saves lives. The same is true for the fifty-five multilingual state members of the African Union, and indeed for members of the Russia-aligned Collective Security Treaty Organisation.

Put simply, the greater the distance between (a) a threat and (b) where I know my people to be, the less importance I place behind the urgency of that threat. The closer a threat is to my tribe, the greater the importance that I place on that urgency.

Hurricane Sam, the Category 4 storm in 2021, was roughly 900 miles from a US coastline. Though featuring on weather bulletins and causing swells on the American coastline, storm force winds affecting Caribbean communities would have been a secondary consideration to most viewers. To Americans, the event caused little more than curiosity over whether this would affect US locations, and, if so, whether TV would stream live disaster footage. In the European media you would have struggled to find any mention of the storm that was, after all, so far from home.

When Yorkshire, in the North of England, was terribly flooded, the London media barely covered it. A month later, minor flooding nearer to London filled the headlines disproportionately. When Germany and Belgium flooded in 2021, and people died, people from the affected regions filled the streets in anger, seeking someone to blame. Few counterparts in French and British cities asked politicians to investigate, and it soon disappeared from their minds and from the agenda of media outlets.

This will change in the space of the next ten to fifteen years, and that change will have an impact on what we consider important. Global issues affecting people far away will start to threaten people we care about through systemic interconnectedness, and they will become factors in our choice of product to buy and company to work for.

We cannot predict which of our people will be endangered, or what kinds of risks they will face. Disasters could be a financial crash driven by hyperinflation, a house price collapse, a new pandemic or an environmental implosion. It could be any, or maybe all of these. Each threat becoming reality pushes our people lower on the rungs of Maslow's Hierarchy of Needs, and everyone hates it.

What seemed improbable in 1990, vaguely possible in 2000, a looming threat in 2010, was a near certainty in 2020. By 2025 it will be a reality, and by 2035 a daily occurrence. In a globally interconnected society, this is our reality. If a disaster strikes one village at a time, it can be seen in houses across the planet. Everyone knows that their tribe could be next, and probably will be.

This is the existential precipice. This is its urgency.
Its proximity to everyone makes this urgency
important to every person alive today.

The mystery of the 'no factor'

Visualising something as being global is far too abstract an idea. It is difficult for some people to guess what their partner is thinking. It can take years for a police officer to accurately judge the mood of a crowd. A great unknown for us, therefore, is how to know what ideas matter enough to become global trends, or even mainstream in our markets.

People globally are closer to you than you imagine.
Interconnectedness is part of the human condition.

Whether you subscribe to evolution or creationism, we all agree that mammals are formed from combining cells in the womb. This bears striking resemblance to the theoretical journey across evolution, where basic elements in our 4.5-billion-year-old planet combined to form the first cells on earth and then evolved through the expanding creation and extinction of species.

Today, there is a beautifully complex and endlessly varied ecosystem of creatures. Each human now accounts for 37 trillion cells. Amid this apparently simple yet endlessly complex reality, a common creation path connects us all. On this basis we can each consider ourselves as being tiny subdivisions of one organism, which I call the global human organism.

Viktor Frankl concluded we are all born with a common consciousness at birth before being conditioned by society. This idea has huge ramifications and explains a lot, such as why humanity moves in patterns and waves, much like mammals and birds move in herds and flocks to join annual migrations that are mysterious, perhaps even to participants.[8]

I confess that I watched a television talent show in the early years of that fad. These shows became the preferred methodology to use public votes to perform market testing before investing in newly discovered performers as mainstream products.

I recall reacting to a facial expression on screen. Perhaps it reminded me of an unattractive personality trait or characteristic. This had the power to change my opinion of a performer I'd previously enjoyed. Within an hour, around 60% of the voting public showed they'd had the same reaction. Someone who had a clear leading position was disqualified.

It seems that ideas become contagion just because we humans react similarly in circumstances, regardless of how unique we like to imagine ourselves to be. This doesn't require media or great leaders to tell everyone what to do. The idea, a reaction, itself is almost universal, instantly.

---

8   Frankl, *Yes to Life – in spite of everything*

In summary, while you observe attitudes of carelessness and lack of activism when issues affect people remotely, the changing nature of threats brings them closer to home. Combined with the immediate nature of threats, we see suddenly increased urgency levels to the point where they can become a more significant priority.

The Great Shift results from a shared awareness of a common threat that affects us all. It becomes visible when urgency makes it so, and the needs that result can only be resolved by each of us making better choices.

3

Tipping Points, Personal And Global

Without defining tipping points for you, I could write, 'Well of course you can't see it; you just need to believe me,' and leave it there. That way, when a market shift happens, I can claim to have predicted it, without specifics.

I will help you to understand why such a tipping point dynamic exists and why it is not possible to define its specifics universally. I will also offer some obvious constants to help you identify where this might affect you.

As I'm distinctly on the amateur end of the spectrum of authoritative sources, I'll keep my explanation generic and will avoid outlandish assertive claims. I can't pretend to be a climate, economics, spiritual or political expert. There are plenty of such experts and amateurs; plenty of data is available speculatively offering evidence of outcomes and timelines. I see no value in condensing this world of data and forecasts for you, even if I were to succeed in making that digestible and entertaining.

My position with regards to the presence of tipping points is that I want you to accept that you neither need nor should seek reassurance from hard data. These tipping points are humanistic, not mathematic. You therefore need to figure out what to watch for; what it means to you when the scenario unfolds one way or another; and to plan how you will act, pre-emptively or reactively.

My aim is to equip you with a lens on your world. I want you to accept the existence of tipping points, identify those most likely to affect you and be ready to avoid them before they arrive. The effects may be in markets, societies or across the world, among those regulating you, buying from you or supplying to you.

We can see the tipping point before it tips

Average people have ideas and opinions on a whole variety of matters. Some of these could influence their consumption, employment and political choices. It is quite possible people hold such opinions for long periods before they act on them, and that might only happen once a critical mass is reached among a population.

Without knowing where ideas originate, some do become viral and have the potential to change the world. The fundamental question is how to predict when it may reach a level of critical mass that's capable of causing a societal phenomenon, and when that, in turn, is capable of causing a disruptive discontinuity in your market.

This is difficult for us to evaluate as individuals. The reason is that while we hear those opinions as they're emerging, we choose to ignore them or listen selectively. For you as a businessperson, you cannot beg forgiveness after ignoring an idea that overnight changes your competitive universe. That would be negligent.

I will demonstrate the effect of this using the examples of veganism and organic produce that are now in shops everywhere.

It is likely that many readers have, at some point, viewed vegans as something of a peculiarity. It has become clear that veganism is more than a choice not to eat, wear or use animal by-products. It has now spawned into a belief system, a movement that values a fundamentalist ethos of holistically better relationships between species.

Years after I became 'vegan-aware', I noticed vegan alternatives on the menu when out ordering a coffee. On Broadway Market in London, I sat down in what I discovered was a totally vegan establishment. We joked, 'Totally vegan, sugar-free, gluten-free, joy-free.' Similar establishments are now located in many streets in most cities and, surprise, surprise, their products are often delicious.

Veganism has now become less an object of ridicule, and more a force to be reckoned with. A significant realisation has been that one of the climate crisis solutions needs to be less meat consumption. As we move towards and past 2050, don't be surprised if your children and grandchildren 'come out' as vegans. The predicted discontinuity in food supply, with alternative proteins and dairy edging towards being a majority in 2030 to 2040, is further proof this is feasible.

In 1989 I met a man who was also an early adopter of the organic food movement. He would drive ninety miles weekly to source organic vegetables and bring them to sell on his street stall, and he was generally thought of as being on the eccentric fringe. I half imagined I'd find him talking to tomato plants and dancing around thorn bushes at midnight. He did do both of those things, but that simply serves to demonstrate that organic produce was then a concept widely associated with outliers.

Today, all mainstream supermarkets stock organic eggs, vegetables, meat – organic almost-everything. Perhaps even the home-delivered bespoke dog food mentioned in Chapter 1 is or soon will be organic.

We collectively tend to ignore new outlier opinions until they emerge as mainstream.

These are precisely the kinds of ideas we ignore at our risk, waking up to find they have changed our competitive markets. Then, we may freely adopt them as our own. Such is the natural human order, our collective brain or the global organism of humanity.

In cases where it takes years or decades for such a shift to occur, there's arguably plenty of time to catch up if you're caught napping – but consider whether the biggest shifts might happen so suddenly that you can't. This is worsened if you imagine that many such shifts may already be taking effect, and you are blind to them.

Although we imagine some ideas to be strange outlier opinions, perhaps they already ripple silently throughout the majority, even if only as a potential. The question is, when does a ripple become a tidal effect?

The inevitable tidal effect

I live on the banks of the tidal River Thames in West London. I'm fortunate to overlook the river itself, which offers a daily spectacle of three different stories depending on when I choose to look.

During the flood tide the water rushes upstream into the channel. This movement becomes so universal and constant that if I only observed the river at that moment it would seem like England might fill up with water. Turning one's gaze at a moment in the middle of an ebb tide, when the river is rapidly draining into the North Sea, one might imagine England is in the process of being drained dry. Similarly, when the tide is turning, its power is magnified, swirling as though it's an unmoving mass of water, home to invisible beasts.

All three states are true at least in the instant when we choose to observe, but the river could be only moments from changing direction and the unprepared and ill-informed observer would never know. At a certain point, the critical mass builds and a tipping point is passed when the whole river's state is transformed.

And... poof. Overnight we become vegetarians.

Alternative proteins are receiving huge investments today. Aligned business models and innovations in areas such as taste enhancements are assembling the building blocks for this to be a mainstream trend. Not many people have seriously considered this new reality in their kitchens, yet experts who predict the velocity of market shift tell us that soon a critical mass will be capable of moving entire industry and consumer paradigms in that direction.

As an inattentive observer, a farmer might be surprised when his market for beef consumption 'disappears as though overnight', just as one might be surprised by the change of tides on the Thames.

We hit inevitability points; that is, a point of no return.
Resisting the tipping point is futile.

These examples – the river and its tides, adoption of food alternatives – demonstrate a natural organic and fluid order that allows us to accept, without hard data, that there is always a point when a small change turns into a trend, and, later, a tipping point when the trend becomes mainstream. If the trend doesn't reach that critical mass, it won't pass a tipping point into mainstream. Sometimes we know deep down that mainstream is inevitable; at other times, we're not sure. We really need to concentrate on prediction skills: monitoring scenario variables to know for sure.

A change in what is universally considered 'truth' does not happen in an instant. That consensus shift can go unnoticed for a long time because the nature of ideas and opinions is fluid. Consensus itself is not like a light switch. As in the movement of crowds, an outbreak of applause becoming contagious, changing tides on the Thames, changes of season and food production, it is gradual, until it becomes accelerated.

In the flow of our shared consciousness, our collective opinions and shared ideas may appear to be disconnected or random until a trend becomes mainstream and we settle on a new truth. Only then is it obvious that a tipping point has been passed. The best one can hope to achieve is to be attentive, and not to ignore signs that are revealing and forewarning of a shift.

We can't predetermine what level is enough to be critical mass for a tipping point. It varies for each change in the direction of motion, be it physical or attitudinal. At some point, however, change becomes inevitable and irreversible, and the mainstream mass joins in with that new direction, or new truth.

I have experienced setting off in the wrong direction, choosing the wrong moment to enter the river. One moment playing in the swirling water, I was caught by an unexpected opposing movement of such great force that I could not paddle back home. I had no choice but to go with the flow and eventually carry my kayak ashore. In business, I have lived through missing a market shift in demand, feeling like I was selling steak at a vegan conference, and learned to avoid it happening again.

I don't know when, but there is a point in the changing tide when the momentum in movement of its mass becomes too great. There's probably a mathematician with an equation or two that could define this. I don't need that level of precision, just awareness. In the river, every molecule is compelled to move in unity; of one mind. An unknown percentage of the water is a critical mass that causes this change. Persisting is a waste of energy and achieves nothing; it can even result in moving backwards.

Think this over a little, and you'll be able to relate it to an experience in business. Consider what happens at a moment when human collective consciousness kicks in and causes people to follow a change in direction or attitude:

- The majority goes with the minority of nonconformists or contrarians, or at least reconsiders which is wrong or right.

- The majority will contemplate whether to press ahead with their original purpose or approach or accept this is the time they will change.

- For the majority, the change becomes an inevitability and no longer a choice.

This all implies a social effect, a 'tidal movement', without need for a predetermination or regulatory change. The same is observed in outbursts of unexplainable applause or cheers in audiences. There's no cause or purpose for this, other than the attraction of a critical mass among them.

It makes sense that a critical mass tipping point level does always exist. It makes sense that it would trigger a shift in the opinions and actions of the mainstream, in any market. My point is... the critical mass is approaching.

Experts predict alternative dairy will hold 60% of the market share by 2050 and plant-based, cultivated and fermented proteins will hold 40% by 2040. That could be the critical mass that affects humanity globally and imprints a new paradigm onto agricultural supply industry. For instance, if too few beef farms have survived, that may reduce supply, increase pricing and lead to even lower beef consumption. We don't yet know when that will trigger a pan-sector extinction event for those who fail to adapt, but, at a level yet to be determined, it most likely will.[9]

---

9   Dongoski, 'Plant-based protein predictions'

It begs the question of us, in all circumstances of life, 'At what time, and with what percentage, could a small change gather momentum to reach the critical mass of movement needed to change a majority?'

The inattentive mind can be taken by surprise. Only an hour before the mainstream changed direction, all material evidence would tell us that no change would occur, the river remaining still or else moving in the same direction forever, and burgers always made with meat.

Arguably, the drastic events that unfolded internationally after the Russian incursion into Ukraine in 2022 were not isolated occurrences. A shift in global human perceptions and tolerance of Russia had been building up, even accelerating, over twenty years. At the time of the invasion of Ukraine, the average person might have been taken by surprise by the ferocity of actions against Russia taken so swiftly by governments and businesses, and how the public opinion of billions swung so severely within a matter of days.

In January 2022, the scale of change that would happen in February 2022 would have been practically unforeseeable. It was the Russian incursion into Ukraine, the straw that broke the camel's back, that caused all manner of change. Who could have imagined the willingness of hundreds of millions to accept hardship to punish a country far from home, and the movements in international politics, banking, trade rules and military strategy, and in competitive markets where companies raced not to be the last to withdraw from a market, fearing brand damage?

That is precisely how tipping points happen. The 'Russian issue' had seemed to idle observers to be a non-issue until the final moment. Then as we tumbled over the precipice at our tipping point, we all realised that we'd somehow been prepared for such action. Until that tipping point, there had been no reason for many to suspect such a severe and immediate shift would be feasible.

Regardless of seemingly enduring calm, tipping points happen. The effects can be ferocious and extreme, such as we may not have dreamed possible. Unexpected as they might appear, if we look deeply at the underlying conditions, we'll see that, although not inevitable, some events were indeed foreseeable.

I argue that the Great Shift described in Chapter 1, which is already underway, will affect markets as much as, or even more than the events of early 2022.

No 'great leader' or 'genius' is responsible

We are conditioned to accept that a single personality, an alpha animal, popular celebrity or great leader of a nation, is accountable for causing movements by great masses of people. Historians point towards single personalities leading us to war, or to victory and peace. Equally, they point to thought leaders and trends that manifest as if magically to their bidding.

While great leaders do exist and they do have an effect, this does not in itself cause great shifts. These actors in history simply serve the masses, representing the shift in mood that exists in minds across their ecosystem. Their opportunity for greatness seems to rest upon how effectively they aid coalescence of groups into the direction that those groups hungered for already. The desire causes the shift, not the leader.

If you view yourself as a leader imbued with some form of almost mystical power to predict all possible futures and winning responses, bestowing wisdom and strategy from above, you should reconsider. Perhaps you should invert that relationship, seek insights from the ordinary people, open your mind so they can inform strategy.

Our willingness to reward leaders with credit for such genius or influence seems linked to our desire to divert responsibility onto them for our collective failures or wrongdoing.

There is a parallel in the messy, scrappy failing systems of the late twentieth and early twenty-first centuries. We blame others – industry, politicians, advertisers, older generations, etc – for the existence of those conditions. We behave as though some great minds or leaders can save us. We take refuge behind the idea that a good old 'someone' will do 'something' to solve a chronic situation. In this state we alternate, in frustration, between expectation of greatness on the one hand, and exasperation that our leaders are not capable of said greatness on the other. Of course they're not capable.

Externalising responsibility for events in history. The rise or fall of great leaders coinciding with society's great or ignoble deeds, such as the mass murder and pillaging of Europeans by Europeans attributed to Napoleon or Hitler. It's obvious. This is only a convenient distraction from the truth; the responsibility for those acts lies with the millions of people whom the great leaders rose to represent. That causality is a collective responsibility of the masses for their own actions, or for their inaction.

Today, we see a similar rise of nationalism, autocratic personality politics, and gravitation away from seeking a balanced consensus and towards idealism and extremism. Leaders we elect, or promote within businesses, are criticised for lack of intellect, experience or any evidence of genius. Towards these same leaders we appeal despairingly for qualities of greatness, which are of course absent. The uncomfortable truth? Their emergence is evidence of an underlying opinion shift that has reached critical mass, and we are responsible for that.

Consider the rise of Margaret Thatcher, and, today, Brexiteers. The Iron Lady was, and remains, a most divisive politician. She made an indelible mark on British society in the 1980s, in a good and in a bad way. As much as she is vilified, in a democracy there must have been a majority who supported her. Those championing Brexit had a similarly polarising and hefty impact on British politics and society.

Their existence, their presence in society, cannot be the cause of these changes. It was circumstances we had allowed to reach a critical state, and the burgeoning weight of opinion among people that caused the shift. The significance of these factors was ignored until it became the new norm, and the unexpected tipping point of an idea was reached. Neither Margaret nor Boris caused these socioeconomic shifts. There were natural reactions in a collective human organism that caused these leaders to arise and that allowed the ideas they championed to reach their full potential.

Shifts occur when an alternative exists

This might seem to be stating the obvious, yet there is a cynical view that, because most of us persist in living and working in unsustainable ways, we lack the interest, energy or commitment to ever change. In that view of humanity, nobody cares at all about their fellow humans elsewhere, and nobody cares about the oceans, simply because those individuals haven't acted yet. That view is shared by my baby boomer friend, who believes change will only happen when it is forced, originating with regulatory or legislative steps. I wholeheartedly reject this.

Many times in life I've steadfastly refused to change, yet only years later, after I followed the critical mass into mainstream adoption, I writhed with embarrassment, even shame, that I did not change sooner. I am not unique in this, so please consider if that shift is triggered by peer pressure, by regulatory change or simply if it could be an organic shift that we all respond to in a swarm-like effect.

Many commentators who are far better versed than I have explained that the pro-Brexit groundswell was not all due to the masses having a well-informed understanding of the EU. Many who voted to leave would have been net beneficiaries had the UK remained. Some who voted to remain never fully appreciated the validity of the arguments to leave.

Brexit is not just Brexit. The vote became a channel for people to vent their feelings of anger and disapproval, at the political and economic system and the situation in general. A tipping point of disenchantment had been reached and the majority followed the alternative that was offered. This was fuelled by savvy marketing that attached a political contest to the issues that people nationally cared about at a human level. The marketing didn't often address factual features but invested in various beliefs on a whole range of issues, many that were not particularly affected by the outcome of Brexit voting. When presented with this being *the* alternative, it was Brexit which people embraced.

We might wrongly presume that the masses are willing to continue in the old status quo perpetually, but that is rarely true. Those who campaigned for the UK to remain in the EU imagined their success was inevitable. The rulers in South Africa under apartheid believed they could depend on a silent majority remaining silent. They were like the supplier of a product used by most people even though it's not good; they imagined the masses would continue indefinitely, even after an alternative arrived on the scene.

This demonstrates that we are wrong to assume that the changing disruptive opinions and new ideas are only held in the minds of minorities of outliers. When viable alternatives become available, people are likely to act.

It is better to predict and act soon than to wait and react, and we all need to decide how soon is soon enough. Conversely, we could consider how late will be too late. One thing seems sure. By the time the media, the mainstream power base and politicians begin to discuss topics as being accepted norms, it is usually too late for anyone to achieve first mover advantage.

By that time, the weight of momentum taking us to critical mass in any given shift approaches its tipping point. Tipping points that could well have been inevitable long before leaders spoke openly. Circumstances alone forced them to acknowledge facts and act.

For inattentive laggards, it's often already too late.

Think about housing market price crashes. I have lived through the events of the early 1990s and late 2000s. In both cases, groupthink, or ambivalence to change driven by ambition and greed, blinded people to the truth. The market had become overpriced and needed downward adjustment, and a 'new norm' arose as if by surprise.

Think about the weight of evidence offered, and the power of denial required to cause millions to ignore that evidence. We know that when a house price crash occurs, because of negative impact on families, the ruling political party expects to fail in their next re-election campaign. There is plenty of energy against the natural order to deny the existence of critical mass. Changing tides and opinions will inevitably reach mainstream once critical mass and a tipping point is reached. That inevitability is real across the global human organism despite often being denied or ignored.

To be a nonconformist is to be treated unfairly.

In 2006 I sold my house and made a timely investment in gold futures. My point is not to say, 'I told you so', although I did tell you so. My point is that, at the time, I was accused of talking-up a disaster. It was as though the state of success people imagined to be perpetual was so vulnerable that a few dissenting voices might cause it to topple.

I was accused of being an irrational and uninformed outlier. I was proven to be justified in being a rational and well-informed outlier.

The denials and accusations continued way beyond the point when the tipping point was reached, and a new truth became widely accepted. At first, I was accused of being lucky and smug. No doubt there are some still bearing a grudge because I benefitted while they lost. At that point, I understood that it was simply a new truth that I had observed, and they had ignored: a truth that had existed all along as a potential, and which had simply reached its natural critical mass and passed the tipping point to become a new norm.

In 2022 and beyond there will be many who don't read this book. Thank you to those few who do read it. Perhaps this book will affect your choices about how you will open your mind to listen to outliers, nonconformists and contrarians; to think about the next Great Shift when a tipping point nears; and of course to decide what to do next.

It is likely, however, that only a few will foresee the next Great Shift in the global human organism and fewer still will take steps to prepare and win in their sector.

Even fewer will have the imagination and guts to identify vulnerabilities and create the new alternative that will attract a critical mass movement, leading people towards and through tipping points, to become market leaders of the future. I hope you are one of these few.

In summary, the rational thinking mind likes to believe something when it can be observed. Tipping points exist even when we don't observe them in advance. We can see trends emerging and building mass following, but we don't quite know for sure whether and when they might reach the critical mass necessary for a tipping point to be passed. By the time evidence exists, it is arguably too late.

By enhancing that perspective with subjective reasoning, we can see many such movements around us, each taking shape and building momentum. As a strategically minded leader, you must not push aside such things simply because of an appearance of subjectivity. By the same token, it's not helpful to embrace these ideas without sound reasoning and strategic appraisal. Powerful forces can sweep away resisters in markets, and that happens within a few brief moments, having seemed impossible before.

Forget about looking for a source of central influence, genius or leadership that is deciding which way the world will be guided. Rather, look for the indicators of the way the world is guiding itself and you will find the great shifts that are about to be thrust into the hands of aspiring leaders who spot the value of championing these inevitable movements.

By watching closely, listening to outliers, choosing judiciously which ideas to grasp and acting early, you have an opportunity to offer that new alternative into which the floodwaters of demand will flow.

4

Business, The Vehicle For Global Change

Business, not politics or regulation, is our greatest hope to achieve change at a global scale. This may seem like a bold claim, but it is a valid point.

I was encouraged by Mohammad Anwar, who asserted in his 2021 book, *Love as a Business Strategy:*

> With the right motivation, it is my belief that corporations could solve world hunger, climate change, poverty, inequity, diversity, and inclusion issues, and more because of their vast influence and resources. Corporations exert tremendous leverage on everything in our world, including governmental policies. They have the power to help solve the world's problems. First, though, corporations need to know what's in it for them. After all, business is business.[10]

---

10   Anwar, *Love as a Business Strategy*, quotation shared with the author's permission

Out there lies a potential purpose, greater than profit, that will strengthen your ability to succeed. Alongside that you need to have the models available as tools that enable you to act. Your business and the impact you make are entirely in your hands. I have watched entrepreneurs struggling with employee retention, or not holding traction in markets. When they reveal to outsiders the purpose that is genuinely important for them, it's as though the world is looking at them anew, and people are literally drawn closer to engage around the values and principles they share.

The difference that you decide to make will touch lives. The effect of that impact may cascade to touch many more lives. By revealing your purpose and values, you may influence the choices of others and provoke a greater purpose that others will decide to serve, amplifying the impact of your choices.

Don't just do good things; don't do harm.

Subsequent chapters more closely challenge what the *raison d'être* for limited companies is, not merely for the sake of challenging it, but to illuminate that even this is changing. You and your shareholders will probably be rewarded by markets for positive impact. You will certainly suffer if you fail to reduce negative impact, both by markets and regulators.

It is folly to get excited by claims of positive impact unless you give equal and perhaps greater attention to the avoidance of negative effects. That is especially true if you and your competitors have been at fault and inattentive to that in the past.

I can't imagine a more powerful market message than one demonstrating you are the first to overcome the harm caused among competitors in your market. This isn't just a desirable, 'warm and fluffy' tactic.

If you are first, you will take customers from your competitors. If you are last, you will lose your customers.

This is not encyclopaedic, nor would it succeed if tested by purist or academic scrutiny for thoroughness. That is not necessary for my purpose. I simply aim to convince you of the plausibility of this as a feature in our reality.

In this chapter, I explore the origin and changing nature of companies, and the effect they can have on societies. I also consider commonly accepted global priorities for impact and provide proven models that offer a method to act upon once you decide which imperatives are appropriate for focus.

Lastly, I challenge the 'profit-first, profit-last' mentality in business. You should know that this need not hamper your business success, but aims to release you from an unhealthy preoccupation serving a limited paradigm from the past. Today, leaders can act in ways more appropriate for our future wellbeing and will profit because of that choice.

The priorities of today

The limited liability company (LLC) was defined in law first in New York in 1811 and then in London in 1855. Loosely speaking, the purpose was to personify businesses and allow for debt and profit with limited personal risk. It reflected the needs and aspirations of 1811 or 1855 depending on where you were but does not address all of today's priorities.

This brief timeline is recent in the history of civilisations and commerce. In my lifetime, though, if there's been one constant it is that companies are what they are, and it's supposedly always been that way. Strictly speaking, that's not true at all.

We seldom consider that the LLC is a relatively recent creation. It was we who created this based on the priorities of 1811 and 1855. Key questions for us today are what our priorities are and whether we should reframe the nature of companies to reflect these new priorities.

Before the 1811 to 1855 period, an entrepreneur was totally accountable for all risks in the business. One who failed was likely to be permanently crushed by shouldering all liabilities resulting from the failure. This prevented risk-taking on new ideas and hampered innovation.

In 1811 and 1855 the LLC was a breakthrough that changed the world for the better. This regulatory and legal innovation enabled entrepreneurs and their investors to have a clearly delineated relationship with risk, and with each other.

The relative balance of importance placed emphasis on the interests of shareholders over that of other stakeholders. This has evolved over years of living in that paradigm. I will go deeper into this in the next chapter, but suffice it to say that in our capitalist world we were taught that profit, and by implication the greed for more profit, keeps the system of creation, production and consumption running and growing.

We originated a system to protect entrepreneurs so that they could take reasonable business risk without punitive consequences. Human nature has since morphed this concept. It now provides a shell protecting us from the consequences of a variety of thoughtless actions and from any after-effects of our choices along the supply chains.

An extreme bias emerged that appeared unbreakable, where shareholder value was deemed the only genuine accountability. Profit with a purpose makes more sense now.

In the late 1990s there was a marked shift in the teaching of ethics at business schools. Though we were not told what was right and wrong, executives were being offered new perspectives.

These new questions aimed to achieve greater balance, which would counteract the assumption that in the name of shareholder profits anything was acceptable, no matter how wrong it felt. I cannot say with certainty if this teaching caused a change or signified a shift in general business practice.

Soon, we saw new types of companies emerging with a message of profit with a purpose; some as social enterprises. A set of different legal entity types spawned to facilitate this kind of business operation. This is material evidence of a general shift that has occurred, in the attitude of entrepreneurs and of their investors and consumers.

I'll admit that in the 1990s it would have been difficult even for me to get my head around it. How could I retain professional credibility starting a company for anything other than to focus on maximum profit? The reaction of those around me might have been, 'Why don't you just form a charity?' Twenty years on and that view has changed considerably. In fact, the paradigm is moving.

A new generation has turned its attention to solving the challenge of how businesses can be formatted to better serve multiple stakeholder groups. Perhaps surprisingly for you, this is attracting equity investors who are not only willing to embrace the same ethos but are increasingly insisting upon it, basing their ideas on clear signals from markets that they will soon exclude companies that lack this quality.

In later chapters I will explain that any business will begin to fall behind competitors if it lacks a coherent principles-led purpose and legitimately sustainable proposition.

Government governs, but business unlocks change

We can solve global societal challenges, and inertia in accepting change, through economic stability that provides a good life for all. While government governs, it is only business that can deliver this.

Not many years ago, governments asked industry to bid in an auction to secure 3G mobile telephony licences. This stripped tens of billions from shareholders and employees of telecoms companies. Most failed to gain return on that investment. While politicians applauded themselves for running a profitable sector, business suffered and so did employees and their families.

At roughly the same time, certain governments sold off gold reserves when the gold price was around $200 per ounce. Within a couple of years, the gold price had soared past $800 and was heading towards $1,000. Governments, flush with cash from giving away national assets at bargain prices, claimed they had delivered a new age of wealth.

I argued that these 'successes' had nothing to do with government competence. That public money came from decades of our parents' and grandparents' generations working hard and paying taxes to build stable countries. The real success stemmed from generations of companies that generated wealth, made profit and paid taxes. The salaried staff they employed willingly paid taxes knowing they would enjoy a stable lifestyle doing so.

Quality of life is a long-term outcome
from long-term inputs.

Our daily focus is on what's directly in front and behind, yet the quality of that day stems from many time horizons before and after, and over horizons far from home.

Our natural horizon in business considers how we equip for features and functions of our product or service, whether our offer is cheaper or better than that of our competitors, and how we fit among others downstream.

Looking just over that first value chain horizon, we see that there are many other stakeholders, both businesses and citizens. Studying where we risk our businesses having a negative impact, and where the opportunities are for positive effects, makes sense for a businessperson.

Success may be improved by serving more stakeholders more considerately. When we grasp opportunities to improve impact over the horizon, these stakeholders become new customers or new suppliers, or simply magnify the strength of a brand.

Every family in humanity gains or suffers
through the calibre of business.

The life of every living human is touched, directly or indirectly, by businesses. Outside of communist states, this has been accepted as a truism. Everything we consume and experience will, at some point, have been contributed to by a business, probably several. Even in communism, it is accepted that supply bodies operate in a businesslike way, albeit to deliver to a planned demand limit efficiently and effectively.

Every family will be sustained by the activities of businesses. Even the salaries of those working in the public sector are funded by taxes from companies or people working for companies. The more wages or profit, the more tax is paid, the more public budgets grow, and the more that can be done for societies. The same is true for those who survive on public-funded safety nets, or charity for those unable to work.

While elected officials govern, economies are only fuelled by the success of businesses. If business thrives, economies do, currencies remain strong and the families in those societies can thrive. The opposite is also true.

It's been widely accepted that the UK is so socially stable because a high proportion of the population are in a taxpaying middle class. That majority are just comfortable enough to have a vested interest in perpetuating the society's status quo, but not quite wealthy enough to stop working. In South Africa, this attribute is missing. Great instability came from a burgeoning underclass that by far exceeds the tiny taxpaying middle class. That has created an unsustainable status quo.

Without strong business and economy, a tipping point in the financial wellbeing of populations can trigger upheaval, or potentially revolution. Your actions in your business can and do potentially affect the lives of everyone.

I've seen estimates that when food costs account for more than 40% of average annual income, then a society and its ruling class are at risk of being overthrown. It is said that this threshold being passed led to the overthrowing of governments around the Arabic-speaking world, known as the Arab Spring. You will appreciate, then, the drastic consequences of underpaying for services in developing economies. This is absolutely under your control.

Societies become more stable when people have higher disposable income, in an economy made up of thriving businesses that are well funded with a strong currency and affordability of basic human necessities. Good business is the vehicle that can achieve this.

Bhutan created a method to assess Gross Domestic Happiness (GDH) as an alternative to Gross Domestic Product (GDP) which has been widely embraced around the world. It is no surprise that in global comparison tables the highest GDH nations are usually among the most affluent societies, although that isn't consistent throughout. Safety, freedom, stability, etc all influence GDH, giving us a framework to consider how we might contribute to the overall wellbeing of society in the countries we deal with.[11]

One must not forget that business, and its conduct and success in serving *all* stakeholders, creates a stable ecosystem and is a cornerstone to achieving these outcomes.

The virtuous triangle

Globally, the governments and regulators, our business communities and related human populations form three points of a triangle of influence and impact. Mutually dependent in an interlocked relationship for sustained success, if one point is disconnected from the others, the whole is compelled into compliance.

Anyone can attempt to make large changes: charging more taxes, demanding change to improve our success or survivability. All of this would be equally dependent on these three points in virtuous triangles working smoothly, together.

Imagine a government asking taxpayers to fund more to care for the elderly. You can see how this would fail if care homes provided poor protection and low salaries for essential workers,

---

11   Sustainable Development Goals, 'Gross National Happiness Index'

and shareholders stripped out profits for personal gain. Such an attempt could succeed, however, if the correct balance were struck.

You will hear people arguing that it is meaningless to chase after individual or company-level efforts to solve the gargantuan issues we face globally. It is precisely not my position to argue that companies or businesspeople will solve the crisis alone. My position is that the virtuous triangle will do so, and that the virtuous triangle will only accelerate towards a solution once businesses and businesspeople step in and cause that acceleration.

If you're struggling to find the right questions to ask in your strategy forum, or to think of ideas for changes to champion global and local impact, that can be easily solved. The world has already offered you a perfectly good list.

Don't struggle. Ask the UN and ask people.

Today, there is a huge focus on the environment and climate, but that is not all you could be thinking about. Remember, this is about you identifying the principles you can associate with to stake a claim to the high ground by either rectifying harm done or creating new benefits. Both can be projected as a purpose-led proposition.

This is an opportunity to improve the impact of strategy by asking people from your ecosystem different questions. Ask them to consider where you have opportunities for impact. You could identify changing attitudes, threats or discontinuities that could lead to a sector-specific or pan-sector extinction event. Look far over the landscape, beyond horizons, and consider broader factors than those you'd looked at before.

Resources are various, and it is not my intention to repeat them here. I wish to point out, however, that the potential exists for your business to redefine purpose and to differentiate. The United Nations website contains details of the seventeen UN Sustainable Development Goals.[12]

Ask people around you to apply their imagination to this. Identify where there are things that you do today, or could do tomorrow, that you need to rectify or amplify to create differentiation. You might also find ideas for your business to show impact through purpose, linked to key principles. Achieving pace in this defends you against others beating you to this differentiation and prevents potential substitutes or existing competitors from trouncing you in the market.

In later chapters I will focus on explaining why such considerations are becoming inevitable and business critical. For now, it is sufficient to suggest that you need to have these discussions and do something with what you uncover.

Talking to people should really be a priority.

As an advisor, I have led over 1,000 company-level workshops where we dealt with strategies for investment, major opportunities,

---

12   Sustainable Development Goals, '17 goals to transform our world'

client development, or product/service go-to-markets. In my experience it's rare, when applying strategy lenses, that teams allow time to talk with people, either their own or others from their ecosystem.

I use the term 'people' in the broadest possible sense. For instance, when considering competitive threats we don't tend to ask people about their experiences working in, selling against or buying from competitors. We simply assume. Those assumptions are usually based on a person's own thoughts, the knowledge in the room or within that immediate group.

I will explain how you can use Porter's Five Forces, Value Chain, the Strategy Diamond and Five Horizons. You will see that lack of truly inquisitive discussion will always weaken even the best strategic mind.

Models and frameworks help you take control

I'd like you to have a structured way of doing this, to equip you for business creativity safely contained in a robust strategy process. I don't need to reinvent the wheel by creating new planning or strategy analysis models. You can use proven models but ask slightly different questions. Some of these will seem old-school and others completely new to you, but together they are as powerful as any.

I will describe and reflect on some examples of models being applied usefully in businesses. There are some you might remember that are quite easy to use but have often been forgotten or ignored. I will remind you of a few of the reliable and valuable ones, and I'll provide a couple you won't have seen.

Porter's Five Forces Model

This was documented in the late 1970s by Michael Porter of Harvard Business School.[13] It is special because it balances several influences against each other and allows us to observe how a change in one aspect might affect another area of influence.

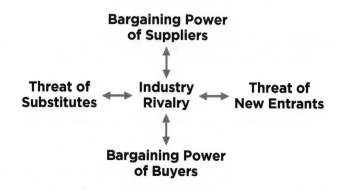

Porter's Five Forces Model

By way of explanation for the uninitiated, Porter reminds us to look internally and then across five factors or forces that affect the business competitively. The five forces are our customers, suppliers, established competitors, potential new entrants and any threat of new substitute products emerging. It is accepted that these forces fundamentally affect how we focus and aim to sustain and grow our business competitively.

Porter's Five Forces isn't meant to be used in isolation. There are guidance and examples in this book on how to use the various models I introduce in an integrated way.

---

13   Porter, 'How competitive forces shape strategy'; Porter, *On Competition*

The good old SWOT analysis and Porter's Value Chain model

From considering the five forces we are then able to examine internal strengths and weaknesses, and external opportunities and threats. I like to enhance this by asking people to think about the impact of not acting upon each item in the SWOT analysis, and to check when it might happen and how to act upon it.

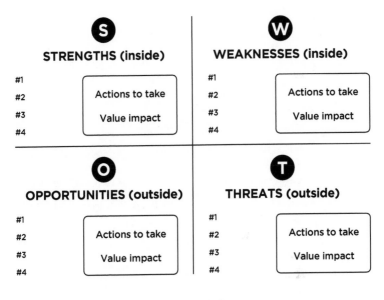

SWOT Analysis

To make this whole process richer, it helps to keep in mind another of Michael Porter's models, the Value Chain, which he published in the mid-1980s.[14] This reminds you to consider all aspects of

---

14   Porter, ME, *The Competitive Advantage*; Institute for Strategy and Competitiveness, 'The Value Chain'

how the business creates value and then capture issues on the SWOT analysis.

SUPPORT ACTIVITIES
Infrastructure, HR, Tech, Procurement

Logistics In, Ops, Logistics Out,
Sales and Marketing, Service

PROFIT

PROFIT

Porter's Value Chain

When you're thorough
then strategy becomes simple.

I worked with an insurance company that decided to repurpose internal software to launch a new software-enabled service in the market. Regular monthly payment transfers from customers were costly and slow. Partnering with one of the major bricks-and-mortar banks, they launched a replacement service that bypassed the payment-clearing network entirely. It quickly gained traction in major consumer-facing companies and became their largest profit source.

I also knew strategy leaders in some of the major banks and in the payment-clearing entity. This was the first time, early in my career, I had seen these models presented in a critical strategic decision. The innovator was a 'new entrant' from an adjacent industry and offered a 'substitute product' – both defined in the Five Forces Model.

While you could be forgiven for suspecting the banks were taken by surprise, they saw it coming. Individual banks knew this new entrant would reduce their income from certain transactions. The traditional banks could have competed, perhaps attacking via banking regulators, but they decided against this.

Refreshing their own SWOT analysis, the banks understood that they had an internal 'weakness' they couldn't solve and faced an overwhelming external 'threat' they couldn't counteract. Rather than confronting it negatively, they sought 'opportunity' to integrate and transform themselves. Focusing on developing a new opportunity in the SWOT, they approached the innovator and secured at least some value from this unforeseen industry shift.

Looking across Five Horizons

You really should be thinking further to new horizons beyond the immediate landscape you have always considered relevant to your business. These can be horizons beyond the current timeline, and horizons outside of your own value chain into that of adjacent companies. Since 2001 I have used my Five Horizons Model to help many executives visualise and achieve this.[15]

One framework in the model provides for five interlocked timeframes and turns your attention to new horizons across future timelines. You will need to have answers explaining where value will be created in each timeline horizon.

---

15   Sanders, www.fivehorizonsmodel.com

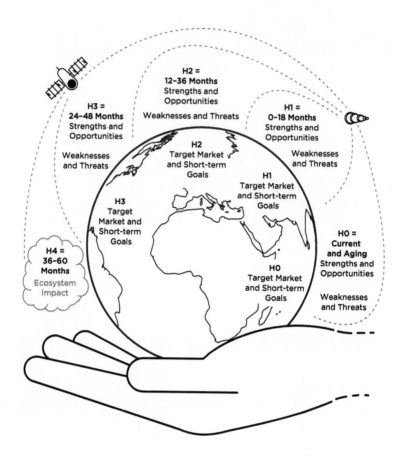

The Five Horizons Model Timeline

The other framework in my Five Horizons Model is an augmented reuse of Michael Porter's Value Chain,[16] which considers five interlocked adjacent value chains, cascading beyond your own normal value chain view.

---

16   Porter, *The Competitive Advantage;* Institute for Strategy and Competitiveness, 'The Value Chain'

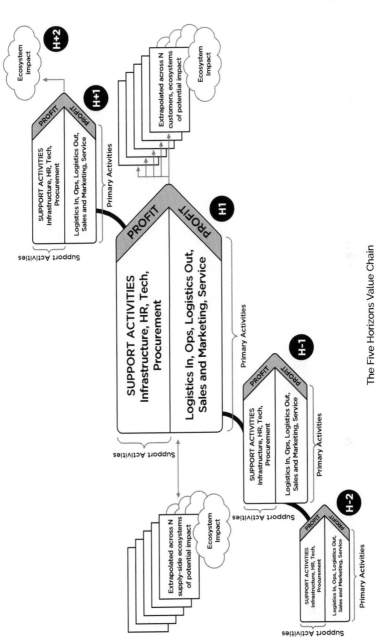

The Five Horizons Value Chain

This provides great flexibility to conceive of where you might interlock with others to find vulnerabilities or opportunities within a few levels of connection – value chains adjacent to your own, in a supplier or customer market.

With the Five Horizons Model, a client was recently able to better clarify when they foresee acting upon market opportunities. Previously, everything had been heaped together, and as a start-up they pointed themselves towards a multibillion market opportunity. Vague at best, it was discouraging investors from backing them.

With guidance in the model, they chose to select two narrow niche opportunities where they felt confident of dominating competitors. For future horizons along the timeline, they provided scenario descriptions of when their other opportunities would come into the frame. That included when to partner or trade sale to achieve scale.

This was strengthened by pinpointing the aspects of that target niche's value chain that would remain vulnerable without my client's differentiated capability.

Rather than working to an artificially strict sequence of timing, they presented a believable scenario map. Trigger points could then be decided based on monitoring external factors and their progress completing internal developments.

Connecting it all in the Strategy Diamond

Donald Hambrick and James Fredrickson provided us with the Strategy Diamond in 2001.[17] This asks us to consider the interlock

---

17   Hambrick and Fredrickson, 'Are you sure you have a strategy?'

of several strategic considerations and is the perfect place to join up insights from analysis using the other models. It is quite amazing to observe how the mind can embrace the big picture in quite simple terms.

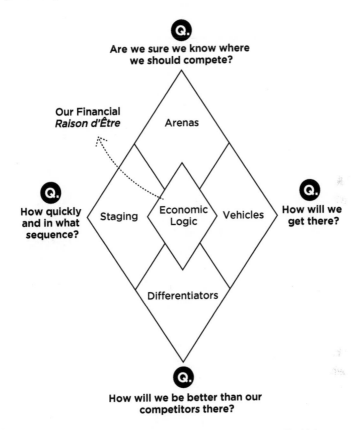

The Strategy Diamond of Donald Hambrick and James Fredrickson, descriptions by Steve Sanders

This model asks you to determine the economic logic of a strategy; the arenas where you will seek to achieve that; differentiation that will cause you to win (or lose); whether you are aligned with the correct vehicles to get you there; and with what pace or staging you can optimally achieve that strategy. As one feature of the diamond changes, the effect cascades throughout, and the strategy rapidly becomes coherent.

The matter of timing, or staging, in the Strategy Diamond can either talk vaguely in terms of years or can be shown as time horizon scenarios. My Five Horizons Model allows you to determine the horizon durations related to the cycles and predicted patterns affecting your business. The 'arenas' and your 'differentiation' there can be reassessed across multiple interlocked value chains. Later in this book, I will go on to offer more detail on the use of the Five Horizons Model.

Getting in a huddle of structure
finds the best answers.

I am a regular guest speaker on strategy to the Master of Business Administration (MBA) cohort at WBS. Each time we use the Strategy Diamond and bring it to life, and people are surprised it's not convoluted and at how simple and powerful a strategy it can be.

I use a live case study of a start-up business I previously advised, and each time, in the space of ninety minutes, I gain huge insight from each MBA cohort. I learn about their team dynamics by observation. I learn to leverage the unique skills and experience that can be uncovered in a room filled with talent. I see first-hand the common mistakes and pitfalls people suffer from in strategic dialogue.

These are tendencies that you should bear in mind when inviting people into strategy analysis. I have found that many tend to limit thinking to what they already know, or to the conclusions they've already reached. This can come from perceptions that a person should know the answers after years in a sector or domain. Worryingly, opinions formed instantaneously are held onto as dogmatically as those that formed over years.

Many also assume that they must act alone, think in isolation and not as a part of a group of minds. Keeping down the barriers of ego is difficult but pays great reward.

Another damaging assumption is that teams imagine they must achieve all the success as planned. They miss the hard truth that opportunities won't remain and wait for them; sometimes it's better to share the load and the gains. Most people I've worked with fail to understand all their sources of competition, what is needed to form a true differentiation and how quickly to execute before others do.

Working with WBS I realised that although my version of strategy recommendation was good, it could always be better. Invariably, it was improved by using the models and frameworks I describe above to gain the cohort's attention and to leverage their know-how in a controlled way that didn't seek to control their outcomes.

You should try this. Extend your group to stretch your understanding of where opportunity exists for impact, hopefully more widely than you'd foreseen. Frameworks allow you to decide how that affects strategy. By doing this with others you will understand a range of new opportunities, and yes, a range of new threats, too. If you avoid involving others, your outcome will be the exact opposite.

A good metaphor is that of a small crew sitting aboard a tiny yacht planning to race around the world. Their captain doesn't talk openly to his crew to ask where they prefer to work, where they can contribute to success or where they could be weak. The technical team ashore hasn't been asked about the maximum safe wind speed for the sails. They are equipped with high-frequency and satellite radio, but they don't use it. They show no interest in where competing yachts are moving to catch strong winds and use the currents. They're not listening to weather forecasts and ignore the rules that umpires have updated one hour before the contest. They just guess. Sound like a good plan?

Extend strategy outreach to the global touchpoints you may impact. Ask better questions and ask the right people. You may find unforeseen parts of humanity you either impact or could impact, positively or negatively. These combine to reveal unforeseen opportunities or vulnerabilities.

A single human being is capable of greater acts when working and living in a collective society, collaborating to magnify success.

You should decide now that your purpose will be of greater impact if it's uncovered by tapping into that strength. This can only be found by engaging the widest sources possible from your ecosystem.

Acting in isolation and ignoring the needs and guidance of others has been proven to lead us into extreme situations, with predictably bad outcomes. Business is increasingly susceptible to the impacts it causes at ever more distant extremes in the world. It stands to reason that, sooner than you imagine, ignoring these global impact factors will become an existential threat for business.

I am interested in how you can act first and engage well, communicate better and learn from that to capture new forms of differentiation. Hopefully, this will create and preserve future competitive leadership.

Act now, or else...

We have looked at how, across the world, people and businesses affect their respective destinies and wellbeing. All businesspeople, not just large corporations, make choices about the products and services they sell, and who they buy from to create those products and services. Though it could be invisible to you at the moment, therein lies your greatest impact potential.

The scale of this among small to medium businesses is truly vast. Five million companies exist in the UK alone, around 17.5 million in the US, 3.3 million in Spain and 2.6 million in Germany. In the UK, only roughly 8,000 of the 5 million businesses employ more than 250 people; similarly, roughly 76,000 are at that level in the US. Most of those millions of companies are small or medium-sized, of course. Each of these has a supply chain they influence and customers who they affect. Most of the 200-million-plus companies globally are also small.

Consider that there are only roughly 41,000 companies in the world large enough to list their shares for investment and ownership on stock exchanges, collectively worth $80 trillion. Whereas the largest companies have tremendous impact, the other remaining c 200 million companies outside that top 41,000 have an enormously extensive reach into communities and families worldwide.[18]

> Business can be an unstoppable force for change or source of intransigence. Strategic choices made by hundreds of millions of us occupying roles in small companies can create a multiplier acceleration effect.

Any decisions taken by politicians, or influence by pressure groups, is minimal when compared to the choices being made daily in smaller businesses. If a regulator imposes a change, it can be adopted, but material change can be delayed for a few years. If a company chooses to differentiate by tuning into a sustainability principle, and 20% of their market is watching for it and adopts it, that creates change instantly.

Imagine I ask you to go out into any community and try to convince 10% of people to never again buy a certain product packaged in plastic. You might choose to refocus them on your insistence on the supplier's ethical employment practices, or another principle of importance and impact.

While I have no research evidence of averages, for the sake of this discourse let's say 2% or 3% make that change. I suspect that a year later only 0.25% would continue, mainly because all

---

18   North American Industry Classification System, 'Custom counts'; National Statistics Institute, 'Spain number of companies: 1998–2020'; Hutton and Ward, *Business Statistics*; Clark, 'Estimated number of companies worldwide from 2000 to 2020'; OECD, 'Who are the owners of the world's listed companies and why should we care?'

available products are wrapped in plastic. Experiments attempted in supermarkets support this conclusion: options for buying vegetables with zero packaging had limited success on the overall use of plastics.

Imagine that three of the four businesses supplying these products into that community together hold 80% of the market share. All three decide to stop using plastic packaging and advertise this to educate consumers and achieve differentiation. In that case, 80% of the community would instantly, and perhaps permanently, stop buying this category wrapped in plastic. There is *no* other vehicle for change that exists today that can achieve this kind of impact.

Nobody is better equipped and has greater influence on consumption trends than the globally pervasive network of hundreds of millions of businesses.

What if you were the fourth vendor and did not discontinue plastic packaging? Almost certainly, your 20% market share would not remain loyal. Many would be affected by a social effect. Observing their neighbours' habits change, and sympathising with principles advertised by your competitors, there is a high likelihood your customers would stop buying your product. If you were the laggard, you would crash.

Looking globally, we can see examples of companies failing in similar ways. In 2019 a Spanish oil and gas company became the first to pledge net-zero emissions by 2050. Around the world others have followed, announcing strategies for sustainability by 2050.

Not long after, a group of petrochemical and fracking companies sued their respective governments and regulators for billions of dollars. They complained that their shareholders had suffered losses due to regulatory changes that harmed the profitability of these inherently unsustainable companies.

Regardless of my personal opinions about these industries, I cannot imagine blaming anyone else for my misfortunes stemming from poor strategy. If I failed to read horizon changes from regulatory or consumer pressure and invested badly because of that, it would be my fault.

Let's be clear, the only reason those companies failed is that they fell out of step with changing public opinion about sustainability. They missed the emerging reality of regulators and governments being pressurised to change rules – the virtuous triangle in full action mode, and business being compelled into compliance.

Let's be profit-focused, by not focusing only on profit.

We have reached a point in history where to achieve a focus on profit-first you may need to adopt an approach of sustainability first or become purpose-led to secure the desired outcome. The profit-first, profit-last mantra might come full circle.

Until now, we've been told that there is too much cost burden for shareholders to pay forward and adapt companies to address the interests of all stakeholders. The petrochemical example demonstrates how damaging it can become to ignore stakeholder capitalism factors, imagining that short-termism would be better for shareholder profitability interests.

Soon you will need to decide where you can sacrifice a little for the sake of investing in principles you know are valued by people in your market.

In summary, looking back at the origins of companies you can see that, while for 150 years the profit-centric shareholder primacy forgave a multitude of sins, this is changing rapidly to a new paradigm. Businesses are uniquely well positioned and equipped to make a positive impact if so desired, and perhaps more so to impact negatively if neglected.

Governments and regulators, businesses and customers will respond in synchronicity to pressure exerted by stakeholders who are increasingly able to dictate terms for the survival of your business. The tools we've looked at here allow you to look beyond the limitation of your own value chain and the current horizon focus on short-term profits. Engaging stakeholders and colleagues from more broadly among your team in a structured approach is a fruitful path to find how your business can adjust strategy according to whether you wish to respond to changes or to lead those changes.

Demonstrating the right impact and accountability will be a necessity to safeguard future company value to investors. No matter how comfortable you may feel that your strategy is correct, and the future is mapped out in glowing lights before you, that sense of comfort is probably ill-advised.

5

Changed Future Purpose Of Companies

Sometimes it's necessary to ask the seemingly unaskable question and to deliver the unthinkable message. In this case, I ask you to examine the facts and consider the realistic prospect that the basis we consider to be the purpose of companies could change, from shareholder primacy to stakeholder primacy, either by force of markets or governance regulations.

If we can't play with these ideas in a book, then where else will it happen? If I were to pose this idea in an online posting there's a chance I'd be subjected to troll-like insults, demeaning my basic intelligence and insisting that everything I say makes no sense.

I realise what I write here will last a lot longer than an online post, and I've dedicated a chapter to this contentious topic – evidence that I feel duty-bound to deliver tough news, even if it is likely to cause me discomfort.

Most people imagine that the realm of possibilities is already defined by our status quo. By that reasoning, in the nineteenth century the concept of a company incorporated with limited liability would never have been put into legislation. If you believe that paradigm can never change, you are badly mistaken – all paradigms can change.

In the previous chapter I gave some background on the origins of companies incorporated with limited liability. We invented these companies based on self-image and priorities, to solve a business need in the nineteenth century. It is time to reimage(ine) companies, to solve a new need that is stakeholder-centric and globally relevant.

Entrepreneurs need to limit their liability, and yet it is already a foregone conclusion that in 2025 other stakeholders will increasingly insist that directors and shareholders accept greater responsibility.

Let's be clear what shareholders want. As with moving market demands, a business leader needs to be well attuned to the shifting priorities of investors. Otherwise, when the time comes to seek working capital for that next big market push or new product, it might be difficult to find.

The reason investors are increasingly studying their portfolio for sustainability and climate impact credentials is not to be nice people, but because they understand that within a few years any unsustainable investments will show lower return on investment. That is precisely because customers and employees want better.

If a trade sale exit or initial public offering event is your plan, it makes no sense to persist in reinforcing 2015 investor expectations. Your 2025 valuation will be affected by changed investor sentiment, and therefore by public opinions that weren't even considered a few years ago.

We have already introduced the recent history of LLCs. Before that, any innovation risk meant entrepreneurs would be risking everything, their home and life savings included. Since then, entrepreneurs have only needed to convince investors, and keep them convinced, confident of a profit.

We can't throw out the good bits. Despite our best efforts with a 1999 start-up for whom we'd created a magnificent platform, the entrepreneur had misjudged the market and failed badly. Owing millions in debt, had this been before 1811 or 1855, with one stroke of the pen that entrepreneur would have been financially devastated for life. In 2001, however, with a company voluntary arrangement, the creditor accepted it was impossible to recover debt and agreed not to enforce. While that venture was destined to fade into oblivion, the entrepreneur later succeeded and retired wealthy.

It's debatable if legislation permitted him to be reckless with others' money, but legislation achieved its aim of protecting the parties and enabling entrepreneurship. It didn't protect his wider stakeholders: the employees who remained unemployed for several months, creditors who lost millions, and my subcontractors from India who had gambled six months away from family delivering services with fees partly contingent on success that they would now never be paid for.

You can decide for yourself. If I ask whether this situation satisfied the letter of the law, yes, it certainly did. Did it satisfy his duty of care for stakeholders, or did it just permit reckless entrepreneurship? I'll let you be the judge of that.

The rise of principles-led companies

In Chapter 1 you read about generational trends resulting in preference for companies that reflect principles shared by customers. I was surprised to see that my own age group, Gen X, has by far the greatest propensity to change brands for reasons of better-aligned values and principles.

There's the emergence of social enterprises, and companies aiming for profit but with a purpose. These were once viewed as peculiar outliers, or experimental with little real impact on market share. I remember one early example and the reaction it caused.

In 2005 a friend from a poor area of the country told me that he was leaving mainstream employment to form his own social enterprise recruitment start-up. His purpose was to reinvest some profits in employability skills. By doing so, he served his mission to fill vacancies, but also satisfied a social principle that was shared among employers and candidates. The brand value he achieved through this was immense. At that point in time, I genuinely did not foresee he would succeed as well as he has done.

The Fairtrade® movement has done a good job of enabling ethical brands to differentiate. You might not at first have believed that a trademark could improve your sales. You might still question the impact of Fairtrade. I checked online, and they report that 57% of consumers globally intend to buy from brands that show a strong Fairtrade commitment.[19] Elsewhere, I've read that whereas only 44% believe pricing is most important, 70% of people

---

19   Fairtrade Foundation, 'Half of global consumers used their buying power to make a positive difference during the pandemic'

most highly value a business that is eco-friendly, gives back to community, or shows corporate social responsibility (CSR).[20]

Whether they be in the mainstream or are new outliers, these efforts signify that there is an attraction among consumers to buying from businesses that are sustainable by design or purpose-led. Speaking personally, the Fairtrade issue has become an important selection criterion for me already, and I can only assume others share this view.

This is not an outlier concept, nor is it new. In the 1980s, in South Africa under apartheid, my father led a CSR programme for schools in South African townships at a local engineering firm. His peers thought there would be only limited positive impact. International investors rewarded this initiative in years to come. Later, several black South African graduates originating from those schools joined his company to begin their career, believing they had shared values.

There is vigorous resistance
among experienced senior businesspeople.

I had a light-hearted debate recently. I argued with a senior executive from industry over the rationale for changing regulations to add shareholder liability for company malfeasance. I was shocked he felt so strongly, saying that doing so would negate the benefit of LLCs existing at all.

---

20   Cox, 'How corporate social responsibility influences buying decisions'

This ignores something that the limited liability paradigm has allowed us to forget. It is only reasonable to assume and expect that companies can and should operate, first and foremost, in avoidance of negative consequences to stakeholders, and investors should be willing to be held to account. Why would it be imaginable one can make profit unless broader obligations to society have been conscientiously fulfilled? Anything less, or so I argued, could be reasonably claimed to be intentional malfeasance or negligence.

A common tactic is to fake CSR credentials
– or greenwash.

Greenwashing might seem to succeed to conceal neglect elsewhere. This is worse than doing nothing at all, falsely laying claim to principles and values that are better embodied by another company.

Consider two businesses promoting fashion products, both claiming sustainability credentials. I know both personally. They are not competitive, but in their marketing messages each claims to be led by their brand's sustainability principles.

The first, UppyBags™, upcycles previously used waste sacking material consisting of plastics that cannot be recycled and are destined for landfill.[21] The production is done by a community workshop in underprivileged Cambodia, where products are sourced directly from the people who make them. A premium price is paid so the community have a good lifestyle, and skills

---

21   UppyBags, 'About us'

transfer gives them a learning opportunity. Products are shipped using surface shipping rather than heavily polluting airfreight. To avoid adding to the pressure on shipping capacity, the company's shipping agent purposely utilises spare capacity in containers that would otherwise have been loaded aboard ships only partially full.

The other company, that shall remain nameless, boasts that its products are produced in the UK and must therefore be sustainable, because finished products are not shipped from overseas. There is no mention of the loss of employment among communities in deprived countries, where people have adequate skills and would benefit from conscious entrepreneurs who could help them learn to produce sustainably. There is no mention of the sources of fabrics used in the production of these clothes, which are in fact sourced from lowest cost suppliers in Asia and shipped by air freight using Just-in-Time sourcing principles, where goods are received from suppliers only as they are needed.

A businessperson can choose to gamble in the hope that consumers remain ignorant indefinitely. Or they could credit consumers with being a little smarter. Of course, not all brands can achieve as much as UppyBags has, but all brands can try. There are countless companies that use tactics like the second company, or even more blatantly extraneous strategies. Meanwhile, there are endless opportunities to make changes, course corrections that genuinely have a more positive impact, and there are rapidly diminishing excuses for not acting upon them.

One must surely see that the sustainability conscious consumer, while a relatively small segment of the market, is studiously well informed. It's true to say that the burgeoning adjacent segment of newly aware consumers might be seeking a quick guilt-fix by buying fashion that has an appropriately greenwashed label and soothing backstory, but that will change.

If the second brand continues these greenwashing practices, it is at their peril. They appear to ignore that consumers tend to learn by osmosis, or the process of gradual unconscious assimilation of ideas, knowledge, etc. Once that transference of insights occurs in a market, the backlash is severe. Having one's trust betrayed is so much worse than falling victim to a simple mistake.

Perhaps there is a place after all for laws that force businesspeople to heed the call to become stakeholder capitalists.

Redefining the company's *raison d'être*

As things stand, regulations in most countries still only oblige directors to preserve shareholder value; for instance, sections 170–177 of the Companies Act in the UK. Internationally, laws only narrowly define responsibilities that are obligations, and all other qualities are desirable.

There is an argument that shareholder primacy is not an issue preventing stakeholder capitalism. The suggestion is that threat of litigation, incentives for being righteous, normal practice and the need to remain legitimate all combine to ensure sufficient corporate conscience. In this explanation, stakeholder interests not oriented by profit will only be served once a company director is at risk of prosecution, in the presence of extreme change to competitive pressures, or in common practice, perception of legitimacy or moral norms.

Today, a company director would be viewed as spending speculatively or wastefully if they invested company profits to prepare for theoretical market shifts. That is especially true of those companies where there is only a hypothetical prospect of this attracting customer loyalty, or of future regulation imposing obligations.

Various forces are at work to change this paradigm. Lobbying top-down for laws to change and a shift in the mood of the marketplace is causing investors to seek transparency, to seek a common measure of the risk that investment values could be affected.

An Institute of Directors discussion panel recently brought together company representatives and legal experts to explore how to lobby government to change relevant sections of the law. There was evidence that companies are already examining how to prepare for an unknown and unforeseeable shift. The risk of any shift being reinforced and expedited by regulatory obligations adds pressure. This has given renewed strength to those delegated with responsibility who, until now, had been out in the corporate wilderness valiantly fighting for this good cause.

I was exploring whether company audit criteria could be extended one day soon, to include companies' environmental, social and governance (ESG) readiness and long-term value (LTV) impacts – 'for societies and economies to thrive, business needs to focus on the long term'.[22] A senior audit partner was supportive but confided that their regulators were unlikely to impose this. There are now frameworks in use enabling large businesses to be transparent, articulate improvement plans and differentiate in the eyes of customers and investors.

---

22 Coalition for Inclusive Capitalism, *EPIC*

Some great work is being done to help companies understand the impact of all this. Considerable amounts are being invested in ESG projects by companies, sometimes by necessity such as regulatory change, and, in other cases, due to directors' awareness of competitive market dynamics and investor preferences. With the scale of capital flowing into companies to support these projects, investors need to see how companies achieve against known ESG performance indicators. They need some means to assess value for their investment compared with traditional ratios. As these practices evolve and improve, this will be more normal for company valuation.

Consider how well prepared you are for when valuation based on ESG impact becomes more of an expectation than something desirable. As I explained to the UppyBags entrepreneur mentioned earlier, in years to come, major brands will need to demonstrate their ESG credentials. I explained how they will seek out alignment with people and companies that have stuck to such principles since their point of origin, with brands that are now recognised for these values and operational norms.

Over lunch, a good friend and I discussed this highly contentious subject. It seems that the legal obligation of directors, and surprisingly shareholders too, for their wider stakeholder treatment may soon be materially changed in case law. Legal thought leaders are beginning to explore how to bring about a new challenge on the paradigm that has pervaded for so many years.

Until now, shareholders have not been liable for the (mal) practices of the businesses in which they invest, which means the shareholder is free to gain wealth, receive dividend payments from the company and sell shares at a profit. When these companies are later found to have been at fault, within certain parameters that are broadly accepted as reasonable, these shareholder gains are mostly untouchable.

There is a strong movement afoot to challenge this. Indeed, there are internationally accepted case law precedents that are already being referred to in legal challenges against shareholders. This could well be behind the recent insistence of investors that their portfolios show evidence of systematic ESG and LTV models.

Soon, not just company directors, but also shareholders who benefit financially, may become more directly and financially liable. It might be fruitless for investors to sell shares and run from obligations to extended stakeholders. It is preferable to sacrifice a little, in a controlled manner, to do the right thing, knowing you'll benefit in terms of brand value and mitigated legal risk.

The message is: think about how to better serve
the bigger-picture needs of all stakeholders –
or someone else will do it better than you do.

Shareholder interests may still be an obstacle

You will be familiar with the financial factors in a business that are seen as paramount to enabling directors to fuel their company's growth. Financing growth is a daily preoccupation for most in business, whether that is by using your own life savings, or by attracting debt finance or equity investment. Proving scalable profitability, and prudent management to ensure return on investment, is generally seen as an important factor that enhances valuation.

There are examples of cases where founders are the only people holding shares. They then can decide whether reduced profits are worthwhile, even temporarily, for the sake of achieving an agreed goal. In these cases, the only concern is whether paused profits prevent continued business operations.

Investment decisions are more sophisticated these days, which is why you've seen high-potential business models that are valued at levels unseen in most businesses. There is a set of characteristics, broadly predictive drivers of future profitability, and these further enhance attractiveness and company valuation in the eyes of investors. These are called the positive discounted cash flow (DCF) characteristics and include aspects of both business and financial models.

While this might sound technical, it makes sense and helps to explain why some businesses are valued at many multiples of revenue, while others struggle to justify 2× profit as their total equity value.

I did a lot of work between 2012 and 2017 using DCF characteristics as design principles, assessing whether businesses can adapt to demonstrate more of the desirable characteristics, and thus increase valuation. It was successful in that it did cause an effect. I experienced a positive impact with one start-up that was orchestrated this way from the beginning. In general, this was hard work, mainly because, to companies not originated with these design principles in mind, it was as though I was trying to retrofit a V8 engine onto a bicycle.

Here is a summary of the factors I called positive DCF characteristics that are known to enhance company valuation:

- Sustainable competitive advantage (hard to copy, relevant to and desired by customers)

- Network effects in the business model (contagiousness of use that is inherent in the model)

- Visibility and predictability (preference for monthly or annual recurring, long-term predictability)

- Customer lock-in, or high switching complexity and cost (not just contractual, but in the mode of usage there are barriers to customer exit)

- Gross margin levels (limited variable risks in cost of product or service)

- Marginal profitability (as revenue increases, the percentage rate of profit grows)

- Customer concentration (mixed model spreading risk across a larger customer base)

- Ease of ecosystem integration (clarity of co-existence approaches within value chain)

- Major partner dependencies (self-sufficiency, allowing for partnerships with rationale)

- Organic demand versus high marketing spend (social or viral effects being better)

- Growth (opportunity, success probability and ability of team to deliver this)

- Risks (resilience of the growth trajectory and mitigation of risks)

- Capital expenditure intensity (eg leveraging software-as-a-service and infrastructure-as-a-service)

- Cash flow/earnings (demonstrated and able to be recreated systematically, of course)

- Total available market (realistic, reachable arenas considering your chosen vehicles)

- Attractive exit scenarios

A key point you will notice is the absence of reference to ESG or LTV. That is for the time being only. I anticipate that ESG and other global impact factors will appear under several of these headings or could stand out as new characteristics themselves.

Don't wait for laws or regulations to change.
Make the shift now.

Aim to keep in balance with global and holistic stakeholder impact to create differentiation and make shareholders happier than competitors can.

Change appears to be inevitable and is visible as early signs of future market pressures. This will be advanced by a global landscape of survival-related priorities and by the interests of increasingly powerful demand- and supply-side stakeholders. This will almost certainly reach a tipping point of urgency within one of your next four horizons for planning, and perhaps sooner rather than later.

Consumer demand is shifting towards a growing preference to buy from companies that echo the consumers' personal principles and priorities. Supply-side changes could become the shift that impacts you most, including either ability to retain staff or sustain supply from suppliers that make up your products and services. Companies further along the supply chain from you who serve end consumers will become increasingly sensitised to these changing market pressures. That could soon create an unmovable force of market demand.

It is only a matter of time until laws and regulations change under the sheer pressure. Remember that the authorities are one of the three points of the virtuous triangle, and they will be driven to take control and help pull us back from the edge of the precipice. Either consumers and businesses will drive the government and regulators in their virtuous triangles to formalise change, which we saw in the case of fracking companies, or forces being exerted in the competitive environment will do it.

Listening to the opinions of experts researching when this issue will mature past a tipping point, my estimation of ten years seems too relaxed. There is a broad consensus that by 2030 businesses will only be able to compete if they can demonstrate plausible ESG and long-term stakeholder value from their business.

Long before regulations enforce that shift, the LTV framework of the Big Four is being embraced by the largest businesses to demonstrate their commitment to move this way. One firm has achieved its own carbon-negative status long before its commitment to reach net zero by 2025. They lead by example and offer clients a realistic path forward. This is clearly a sign of practices that will become pervasive.

Using the Five Horizons Model from Chapter 4, it could make sense to plot a scenario map per horizon, to prepare in advance of a future moment you might choose to activate aspects of this strategy. That will avoid becoming swamped with ESG and LTV demands. This will depend on how you imagine your sector could move.

In summary, your decision to act upon these options sooner might be caused by study of changing demand and the risks to the business of not acting soon enough. Equally, taking rapid action sooner could be a way for you to differentiate and gain market share against less forward-thinking competitors. At least you'll be equipped to make these judgements and decide on a solid basis of analysis which way to move.

Whatever choice you make when deciding how to act upon this, I hope you will agree with me that the option to wait and see is not a good choice.

Act now, use the strategic planning frameworks I have described, and form hypothetical scenarios for your possible next steps. This will allow you to decide later when, and with what intensity, to act, while keeping shareholders as happy as or happier than before.

6

Discover What You Could Be

Learn how to reframe the situation your business faces into a new context better aligned with shaping or responding to these strategy changes, and gradually you will seek out better opportunities to look broader and to create the next reality. Not waiting and reacting but shaping and acting now.

You have read a lot here about changes in buying and employment preferences, and the effect once that change goes beyond a tipping point to trigger pan-sector disruptions. It rapidly becomes the priority to safely navigate this Great Shift, working out how to handle factors largely out of your control, and mitigate threats by shaping relevant propositions.

Regardless of the presence or absence of a Great Shift, this chapter will be valuable. If I needed to choose one factor to unlock imagination in business, it's the one I discuss here, so resolving this issue is important.

The solution, or a limiting factor?

As humans, we tend to create relatable boxes that simplify our world and the work we need to do. On one hand, this is useful as it helps customers more easily grasp the notion of what we offer, and makes it simpler and more relatable for us, too, which is of course desirable in many situations. If everyone were to be off at tangents reinventing and reimagining too frequently, all plans to implement and deliver could be delayed.

On the other hand, once a box is formed it then becomes a limiting factor preventing or delaying efforts to diversify the opportunity, or to innovate solutions. I have observed just how quickly people form their boxes in snap judgements, and in some cases stick to that dogmatically. Even as one sees customer needs evolving, a mental filter only allows us to perceive the solution previously in the comfort (danger) zone, with little consideration of alternatives. This worsens once a person invests their emotional energy to evolve and perfect and thus reinforce their fixed view.

If we are to have any chance of improving the solutions we offer, we need to become more open to the changing nature of the needs and issues we focus on solving. We need somehow to overcome or regulate this human nature limitation. I will use three anecdotes to demonstrate this: from a corporate, a university and a start-up.

Corporate: saving jobs at an old telco

I led a process to find new sources of more profitable income to replace declining end-of-life traditional products. Ultimately, the purpose was to preserve jobs and profitability for shareholders.

Salespeople and delivery managers were deeply invested in the old way of working. They had for so long based their personal value on delivering that way. Their sense of self-worth seemed dependent on existing product messages, ways of selling and features. When asked to have a different level of business conversation with their clients, antibodies kicked in. A collective resistance proved a near impossibility to change.

You may relate to having been in a similar situation. I discovered their resistance was not caused by any resentment of me or the new ideas. It arose from a deeply rooted human trait. They had a strength as a tribe and trusted the weapons that they'd tested in pursuit of income together for so long. Asking them to change was threatening. Intuitively, they felt that changing from their comfort zones would effectively negate their identity and professional value.

When an innovative idea becomes dogma

A London University business contest asked a budding entrepreneur to share, brainstorm, test and improve her business idea to rent fashionable clothing in bundled packages. The aim was to compete for award of funds and sponsorship.

Above all else, this person was convinced they were destined for greatness, and regaled colleagues with tales of public persona and widespread social media recognition. Yet, when tempered by the challenge of peer brainstorming and physical market testing, the group discovered that the idea had quickly moved from an innovation to become a dogmatism. Many reasonable suggestions to course-correct and improve were defied or ignored; for example, what pricing bands would be considered attractive, the quality of clothing, cleaning, packaging and service for delivery, collection and large-scale capital, systems and inventory that would be required.

You will relate to youthful inexperience mistaking single-track obstinance as being admirable persistence and drive. We discovered that the underlying reason was that the entrepreneur had attached the value of personal identity to the irrefutability of the idea. The strength of that student's conviction was that the first solution was the only one worth considering. The group knew that was a weakness but were powerless to force a change of attitude. To the student entrepreneur, it was a strength. Three years later and this entrepreneur has not gone to market, yet major retailers have taken this idea to heart and have started to explore the practicalities of it.

Start-up: missing the gravitational pull

In contrast, there are others who embrace this search for the point of gravitational pull for mainstream success.

I was approached for advice by an entrepreneur who had already built and sold a business, won awards and represented his country as a young entrepreneur ambassador. His aim was to reach a bigger market quicker, enacting an enhanced strategy in advance of an investor fundraising event the next year.

Research and development (R&D) and the soft launch were complete. This business equipped hospitality venues with a technology presenting data online to help a target audience suffering a specific accessibility challenge. Fundraising would be hampered by an inability to secure a critical mass large enough. This demanded a quick move to prove their value was applicable to mainstream users, not just the target niche. This was achievable; indeed, I would be keen to use this data myself. Yet there was surprising resistance when I offered to help unlock a global search engine provider to be his sales channel; to feature this data in map results for venues.

What struck me as noteworthy was that the entrepreneur told me he had already suspected such a mainstream opportunity existed. He saw that potential but preferred to first perfect the big idea upon which the company had been founded, before what he termed as 'getting distracted'. I wonder how slow pace and perfectionism will serve him once competitors notice such a huge opportunity. My advice was to move quicker and capture that space, rather than to hope and pray.

Big ideas misfiring add to the cost of failure.

Reliable research tells us that across a large sample of businesses up to 95% of launched concepts to market (CTMs) fail. In the Fortune 1000 only, this causes a conservative estimate of $60 billion of losses every year.[23]

A senior managing partner at a global consultancy confided in me that during recent years they had been on a campaign to encourage experts globally to create repeatable offerings. Three years on, 2,500 such offerings had been created at significant investment, and nearly all had been bought by only three to five clients.

These CTMs had not been evaluated for scale potential. Their originators were not equipped and did not understand how to make them repeatable by design and scalable with intent. The only remaining option was for me to help reallocate capital so that the best could survive.

---

23   Kuczmarski, TD, quoted by Ulwick and Eisenhauer, JA, as cited by Jones and Knotts, 'Factors affecting innovator success and failure'

I've invested considerable time and effort in building a CTM model framework. The aim is to allocate capital investment based on objective measures that are predictive of success. This defines what all ecosystem players need to do to achieve maximum CTM success rate and accelerate time-to-market and return on investment.

I will go on to explain why this issue exists and why my solution is required. This is, once again, a manifestation of the weakness in human nature. We evolved socially and intellectually with the tools to thrive as individuals within small, easily relatable units. We didn't evolve to handle complex multidimensional, wide-ranging business systems.

Most people, possibly all, will default to a habitual pattern, reverting helplessly to their closest intimate group. In the case of deciding the best concepts to take to market, this causes people not to address the complexity of the whole business system for that decision. The cost of evading complexity is so much greater, and the damage caused is longer-lasting.

The tendency to focus on the first obvious issues and solutions risks one failing to visualise wider customer vulnerabilities and opportunities. That is especially true when issues are more abstract across a whole system. You may remember instances when suppliers raced to fulfil specified customer requests, never questioning what broader value drivers there were. That is why cross-selling and upselling fails because people don't seek to contribute more widely to tackle unstated customer value drivers.

Consider the issue of making snap judgements. Most harmful is when the precept of a lasting proposition is formed rapidly and is later worsened gradually as it becomes entrenched as habit over time. There is a risk of this being your 'innovation that becomes a dogma'. That is when you develop dependence on ideas that can be detrimental to the greater good. It leads you to ignore broader relatable requirements and miss new options for cross-selling to make greater impact.

Working with Stephen Chadwick recently, I saw how the strength of his leadership and presence of mind enabled him to decisively cast aside such assumptions. His openness to pivot, and gaining board approval to do so, allowed him to direct the minds in his company to set a new course. The business was able to make a step change taking it closer to meaningful competitive advantage. Persisting on their established path would have resulted in frustrating near misses from direct sales situations. The course correction they achieved allowed them to find their most attractive go-to-market and partnership context.[24]

There is an inherent human bias at play here. You will naturally prefer to support concepts that reaffirm an existing viewpoint you hold, and that come from people who are like you or who share a common background to you. This results in a reluctance to just say 'No', losing the power of using structure to decide whether no is the correct answer. The power of no in this context is immeasurable. It saves avoidable sunk costs where CTMs should simply not be permitted to move forward. It prevents you, me and everyone concerned from being distracted from achieving value elsewhere.

The impact is worsened by the fact that the best ideas could be ones that you don't perceive positively. They might contradict your viewpoint or could come from someone so different to

---

24   Referenced here with permission

those you respect that there seems no way of reaching common ground. That is a flaw in this situation that we need to solve. In later chapters we will look more closely at the interlocked strategic processes this requires.

The necessity of creative thinking

Looking back at most of my work, there is one commonality throughout. I often became a chief contrarian, asked to introduce ideas into the mainstream that may at first have been completely at a tangent from the core. I was known for being a polite but robust nonconformist, because for a while at least that was required to advance change rapidly. Fortunately for me, I mostly chose breakthrough tangents that eventually succeeded.

While many people might omit to credit me, these initiatives led to a positive and stable future, one that often benefitted those who threw rotten fruit from positions of safety inside the core. I braved the storms leading those unpopular tangential paths.

I have enjoyed it thoroughly but have no illusions over why it was so difficult. It had to do with how unpopular one becomes as a nonconformist contrarian. People don't like it when you challenge the established comfort zones they've learned to value. It seems they value these comfort (danger) zones more than they fear the threat of extinction in the workplace.

Here's a story to make the point. Let's say the future of shipping relies on carbon-neutral power for companies to remain afloat. It stands to reason somebody needs to stick their neck out to press that forward. That means they don't just need to come up with the idea, but they also need to experiment, prove it and go mainstream with it.

Enter, stage left, the 'tangent team' who mostly act as contrarians to the core model and core mindset. They are mostly disliked or mistrusted for that reason.

These are among the most valuable people, and they are sometimes found in start-up businesses, often inside but adjacent to the core in large enterprises. I've spoken to a lead entrepreneur who takes on this unpopular role himself so his whole team can remain entirely focused on the 'as-is'.

Outliers sense repulsion from the core.

In my story, a cargo ship will have a crew whose careers have been invested in perfecting the running of a slick oil-fuelled giant of the seas. Theirs is a life of direct accountability and no-nonsense. The captain and senior team must keep them focused so that the ship fulfils its purpose, in as straight a line as possible, with least fuel, in the shortest time.

Imagine they've set off to enter the Suez Canal in four weeks. There is the crew, watching overboard, perhaps hurling jocular insults. Four valuable colleagues take provisions into a small boat covered with solar panels to set off from the ship. That tangent team is on a wacky race to reach Suez before the main ship can. On the cargo ship, even at the most senior level and perhaps the captain too, there will be muted complaints. This is wasting time and money and distracting their people from the real job of getting a giant diesel-fuelled ship to port.

Sometimes a common approach to work
becomes a destructive groupthink.

Do you recognise this reaction, perhaps in a parallel that you've observed in business? I do. Once upon a time, before services became a normal line of business, there was a fictitious IT company. Any resemblance to a real company is purely coincidental, as this is in fact a combination of several experiences. In my story there lived a young man who was the first ever sales manager of professional services. Let's call this fictitious company 'ITCO' and our hero 'Todd'.

For six months Todd received threats of a short-lived career. Warnings of, 'Boy, listen here, we do not charge clients for service.' In meetings, Todd was told, 'Boy, sit down, shut up and you might just learn something.'

Years later, our hero Todd would lead another industry-first transformation, moving ITCO's mid-market machine from a small direct sales team to a mass custom solution go-to-market engine making several hundred million a year. In both situations, imagine how many ITCO people would have been like those attached to a diesel engine legacy on board that fictitious cargo ship.

There's a good ending to our story – the ugly revenge scene. The dinosaur who made the 'sit down and shut up' comment was made redundant six months later. He was the 'old elephant' and in his heart he firmly held onto sentiments such as 'the old way is the best way' and 'if it isn't broken, don't fix it'.

Our happy ending? ITCO would soon boast that most of their profitable revenue came from services or was from lines that were led by services. The new value-added solutions context Todd fought to establish had then aimed to secure new customers for ITCO's traditional products and partner products. It was not long before everyone became firmly secure and dependent on that business model.

Of course, Todd lived happily ever after. Isn't that how all fairy tales end?

Vulnerabilities of greatest impact can be solved anywhere across the whole ecosystem.

I've explained our natural affinity is with easy-to-grasp boxes and our preference is to reinforce established beliefs. This can cause value propositions that are rooted in only the most familiar areas of your impact or features. In preferred boxes we tend to look no further than the issue that was solved at origination of a product or service.

Persisting with doing things the old way, until proven wrong, becomes a harmful, self-limiting factor. It restricts those involved in go-to-market planning, sales and delivery. The danger is when one doesn't revisit, challenge or stretch these assumptions, nor seek ways to reach beyond established norms.

The further you expand your search for new ways to make a positive impact, the more appealing and stickier value propositions become. Don't leave it up to customers to discover these new uses and value opportunities for themselves, because they most likely will not be so helpful.

Experience has given me many examples of salespeople who dance around the edges of customers' changing issues. They describe features and advantages yet hesitate to take the leap of helping that customer translate these generic ideas into impact statements. Invariably, that is where value is created by customers and most surely carries more weight in the customer's mind.

Chances are that the greatest areas of impact would go untouched because of lack of awareness, or simply lack of mental energy applied. The failure is from the inability to translate one's ideas into how customers will create quantitative impact. This is a great pity. Yes, sales performance suffers, but the greater pity is when potentially valuable benefits are missed by customers across the market.

I have facilitated more than 200 strategic market or client development processes focusing on solving this issue, which demonstrated this perfectly. Teams consistently struggle to form imaginative differentiation and lack ideas that can impart client urgency for their strong points.

In these workshops, I first asked groups for their greatest competitive strengths. In larger businesses this always included, 'Our breadth of portfolio offers more attractive products or value-added capabilities than any competitor.' In smaller businesses, common answers were 'our product is higher quality' or 'our solution is proven to deliver more benefits than any competitors'.

When the time comes for teams to articulate propositions, they most often repeat previous failing proposals. Often they ignore wider portfolio options. Almost always they only connect solutions to the most familiar benefit ideas. They also miss the chance to explain that the product doesn't deliver value but creates new capabilities in customers that the customer can then use to reliably create value. Most vital of all, they don't understand what makes something urgent for customers. You may be correct to ask how on earth they sell anything. The answer is, 'Only with difficulty.'

To get under the skin of this, first one needs to acknowledge that breadth of portfolio, and one's generic ability to enable value, is meaningless if not in a customer context. Ergo the need for techniques and approaches to get better at attaching to this.

The enlightenment moment? When teams reflect on finding the greatest possible vulnerability that their capability can solve. The winning formula is to show clear understanding of those vulnerabilities and help customers articulate how this broader set of capabilities can achieve rapid and high levels of positive impact. Go-to-market traction is greater when you spell this out for markets, as with individual customers.

Granted, companies devote months of induction to indoctrinate staff in code words and product descriptions. After overcoming the resulting inability to think outside those boxes, by far the greatest challenge is to give people confidence they are permitted and well qualified to challenge customers. You want customers to abandon preconceived ideas of 'the best approach to gain value' and attach to the need for a broader approach to add greater value in unforeseen ways where you're differentiated. Both must happen to achieve the best for yourself and customers.

Examining the interconnected value chains of your target market, as per the Five Horizons Model introduced in Chapter 4, allows you to find ways in which your capabilities can create new threads of opportunities. This should be expressed as enabling customers to acquire new capabilities and thereby create new value.

Even when a customer is an end consumer that you'd normally consider to be in the last part of the journey, that's not so. Consumers serve employers, families and communities where your impact could be translated into differentiation. That is the opportunity to become a true challenger of assumptions which have until now limited a market's or a customer's ability to achieve true scale of benefit potential.

Talking in 'horizons'

Chasing the next month's target makes it difficult to think this way. All energy and intellect risks being absorbed by selling more of what's on the shelf or the bench. Yet somehow, to make maximum impact on LTV and company-level valuation, you need to think further and broader, and act with energy to win better.

It's futile to sideline important value creation because it's not delivering today.

Back in 2001 when Five Horizons was first used, I was pushing the boundaries of where colleagues and clients were willing to invest their time. People, it seems, are relentlessly occupied with this year, maybe next year – so much so that they may even turn hostile if someone asks them to use time discussing the future, otherwise rather coldly labelled 'silly pipe dreaming'. A frustration for me, as you can imagine, was that my futures and pipe dreaming frequently underpinned the continuity of their employment only two years later.

I needed to find a way to provide them with a rationale as to why something deserved their attention when it might only come to life in four or five years. It struck me that whenever an individual was assigned responsibility for this, they almost immediately fell a couple of rungs down the cultural and political pecking order.

There can be no doubt of the importance of developing future value creation to maintain company stability; however, that positive impact is way out there in Horizon 3, 4 or beyond, which results in those responsible being relegated down the layers of influence. When the time comes for deciding who has the biggest voice at the table, deserves greatest urgency or is entitled to claim available capital, the further out your 'impact horizon' is, the lower the priority you are given.

Unsurprisingly, you might have seen the most experienced and skilful people avoiding these long-range initiatives, precisely because of the loss of status and probably loss of income that often results. The captains of these tangent teams, and the companies they supported, needed a means to visualise and collaborate for the future with equal authority to those pursuing today's targets.

As described in Chapter 4, my Five Horizons Model is for those who want to treat future horizons of impact with an appropriate level of importance and urgency.

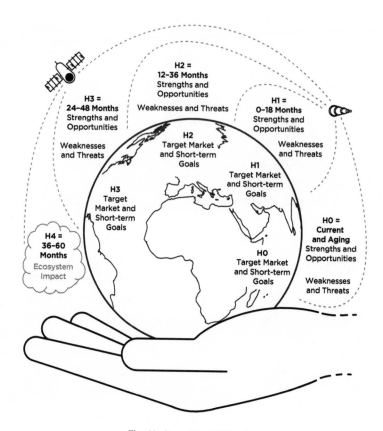

Five Horizons Model Timeline

Illustrated as a picture of the earth's surface resting in the palm of a hand, the viewer's eye sits at the right of the planet and sees Horizons 0–4.

Horizon timelines are adaptable to your reality. Typically, H0 deals with the present conditions as they've existed for the previous twelve months. H1 is the first phase of twelve to eighteen months, and the subsequent horizons cover between twelve and eighteen months each, perhaps with a little overlap. An orbital satellite with a reflective dish is to the left as the only way to see what is over H3 and H4 – better than a crystal ball, I think.

The purpose is to pinpoint plans that will provide value delivery of highest impact in each. H0's engine might be in decline. Additional propositions or planned impact areas may be launched for each horizon, and the SWOT and contribution forecast later examined. It's helpful to decide conditions that you'll monitor to decide when to activate a proposition or a plan. You should run a discovery process to reimagine sources of opportunities or redefine your portfolio, and perhaps create new concept-to-market projects.

As explained previously, the Five Horizons Model is broader than the timeline, and encourages exploration further than one's own value chain to find vulnerabilities or opportunities to solve. Pick any point of your value chain – let's say, for simplicity, one of your suppliers – and you can see that they too have a value chain, and suppliers and customers. Then those third parties also have other suppliers in their value chain. Via interconnections we can contemplate a greater range of activities, vulnerabilities and opportunities in interlocked value chains.

Look at the customers in your value chain, and already you can see that they too have customers whom they influence and to whom they try to offer differentiated products or services. If serving consumers, they will have employers they need to impress who, in turn, may themselves be greatly influenced by those employees.

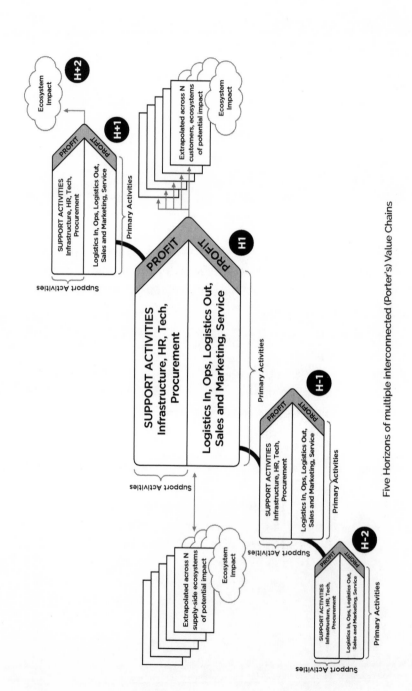

Five Horizons of multiple interconnected (Porter's) Value Chains

Already, then, through this simple perspective you can investigate how your business impacts five different value chains. You can search there for possible value and impact, and urgency, across all aspects of all five. That is the second approach to using the Five Horizons Model for strategic consideration and stretch potential.

People know what they can see and touch,
but imagining feels weird.

Typically, executives are preoccupied with, and feel most confident about, H0 and H1, yet, even when discussing H1, which is relatively near-term, they may lack the certainty one would imagine. The Five Horizons Model insists that no blank spaces are acceptable. Gaps equal strategic vulnerabilities. Soon it might be too late to start doing anything about them.

I have observed that clients appear nervous, as they have never been put on the spot so deliberately about something that they don't yet understand fully – that is, the future.

Create a safe space and provide a reasonably clear purpose for discussing hypothetical futures. Accept that the process will only be truly valued by teams after they complete the process. People often consider the exercise to be escapism, or perhaps that it should remain in the realm of product managers or some faceless 'strategy lead'. I compel people to accept that there is nobody else who is better able to handle these challenges than they themselves. I encourage them to stay the course, complete and execute.

Initially a brief exercise, one might easily walk away somehow satisfied. It feels like an interesting experiment to create a thought-provoking view of what might be achieved in the future business. It is vital, at that point, to embed this model into the core conversations of the business.

Every question, all incomplete answers or assumptions, need to be ironed out as a matter of priority. It makes little sense to persist pushing and delivering daily if you're headed in the wrong direction. If a clever strategic choice could unlock company-level value, that makes all your efforts more lucrative.

Let's refer again to the hypothetical examples of the international motor car company and hotel groups I first referred to in Chapter 1. Each country's leadership team has a mindset firmly rooted in the paradigm of building and selling cars, or filling hotel rooms and restaurants. I can say from experience that they will be suspicious and closely challenge each digital innovation's validity, causing huge delays in go-to-market and risking loss of potential differentiation.

After taking the horizons view, it is evident that in H4 this company need no longer depend only on selling metal boxes on wheels, or filling hotel rooms. Though there will be manufacture and accommodation, it will be a small part of the ecosystem value opportunity. Future leaders of those sectors will provide a digital experience enabling consumers to gain the experience that they need – be it mobility or a relevant travel experience – of any kind whatsoever, whenever and wherever they need it.

The headline strategy says, 'we will be a mobility company' or 'we will provide travel experiences', but that will make little difference to their Horizon 0 and Horizon 1 attitudes and their activity in operations. Only by applying the Five Horizons may one provide clear visibility of rationale for the steps needed in H2, H3 and

H4, which become part of the generally accepted way forward. In cases where I have applied this approach, those in the core mindset are now executing accordingly.

In a data compliance technology firm that I advised, an investor pitch deck showed a confused basket of ideas to investors that did little more than portray founders as excitable. You might have seen similar things before. I spotted 'alliances with security distributors', then 'AI software development, partnerships and acquisitions'. Of course, then comes a grand finale we so often see: 'exit through trade sale'. All that alongside a list of more standard day-to-day services and go-to-market opportunities.

The Five Horizons Model became a focal point for the leadership team and founder to realign their thoughts. As soon as they settled on having told a good-enough story via the horizons, I would, of course, challenge them to go deeper and show evidence, facts and serious thought being applied to these otherwise loose-lipped headlines.

It was crucial for that team to express all aspects of their strategic ambitions, but to do it sensibly, showing sequence, cause and effect, and dependencies. Flow from one to the other then sensibly set the scene for key funding events that would be required to deliver at each level. Most important was the effect on how they moved into implementing strategic conclusions. Investor sentiment was positive.

When planning horizons, examine scenarios
to avoid missed timing.

It is entirely up to you whether to be alert and prepared, or to wait and see. If you act, experience shows outcomes improve after involving people with their fingers on the pulse of customers and markets. Faceless strategy people and product managers don't do well when at liberty to act independently. Collaboration with those who live and breathe within the markets is vital.

In 1997 in response to the Kyoto protocol, diesel engines were promoted as being environmentally friendly. Of course, there was plenty of information available in the automotive sector that this misunderstanding would be short-lived; consumers would soon become better informed.

Strategic investments to launch fleets of electric vehicles (EV) were made during the 1990s after the initial success of General Motors, intensifying in the 2000s. Tesla was formed in 2003 and launched its first car in 2008. The timing was not driven by regulatory change and consumer pressure becoming insurmountable but is a sound example of a Horizon 4 strategy receiving investment according to the scenarios as that industry predicted they would unfold.

Governments and regulators picked up the trend that was initiated by business and intensified by the influence that several innovative businesses exerted over consumer opinions in a changing generational profile of society.

There are car companies classed as laggards who failed to activate a variant strategy based on evolving scenarios. They opted to dismiss EV and depended on diesel engine product strategy. Among them is one of the most prestigious British car brands. They are accused of promoting biased research and misinformation that EV will never be as sustainable as combustion engine cars. They fell into the diesel engine trap and are squirming and protesting to the end.

There is always a choice, and it's better to make the right choice at the right time.

In 2000 there was a head of steam building up towards banning cigarette smoking in drinking and eating hostelries. During the years leading up to the 2007 ban in the UK there was a powerful lobby insisting there was no substantive health risk to smoking in those venues and that the ban would, instead, have an unacceptable impact on personal freedoms.

Of course, some owners of hospitality chains took a 'wait and see' approach, while others prepared well in advance. In 2005 the possibility of a smoking ban was a Horizon 2 strategic factor, and it was wrong to ignore that. Those who planned in detail activated plans just before regulatory announcement. They scored significant brand- and market-share advantages compared with the laggards.

It stands to reason that planning forward in the horizons is a valuable way to allocate your attention and investment. Then you may deal with planning how to message stakeholders in a well-considered and proportionate way about what comes next, then after that and then maybe even after that. Emphasis is on building brand value, capturing market influence and securing leadership based on your foresight.

You decide the audience and your messages

As two younger generations age and become the new twenty to fifty age group, they will carry the greatest spending power and workforce influence. There is a lot at stake when deciding how to investigate and act on implications of this Great Shift.

Literally, you can stall and inadvertently become the villain. Remember those petrochemical companies suing governments and regulators in sullen fits of rage having seen their plans crumble because the world decided to change opinions.

Equally, your decision can pitch you as the hero. You can be at the heart of a movement in whatever principles-led market shift you elect to attach to your purpose.

Your message can leave you scrapping it out among the 'features wars' where customers are left with no option but to buy cheapest. With vision and purpose, you can provide customers with that principles-led alternative that they have been waiting for. Their transfer of loyalty may be towards you.

Curate your message carefully at every step or risk being a brand victim.

There is an international car company who shall remain nameless here who have long since been ahead of the curve in environmental credentials. Their strategy since the mid-1990s has been evidence of this. They are absolutely one of the heroes, not the laggards or villains clinging to the past.

Their genuine belief is that it's better to take a little longer retiring combustion engines to refine new technology, hydrogen-fuelled perhaps, that will offer more advanced sustainability than EV. A board member unwisely spoke out to the press. He challenged governments to delay bans on combustion engines. Surely, or so he reasoned, it's better to allow a few more years of R&D to create truly sustainable mobility. Though well intentioned, it was a terrible misjudgement.

As major shareholders joined a chorus of public abuse, it struck me just how fragile such a reputation can become with poorly chosen messages. We will soon see their leadership re-emerge by launching net-zero vehicles such as hydrogen-fuelled, or even vehicles that make a carbon-negative impact. With consumer digital advancements they may enable a future where people never own vehicles, optimising the use of mobility options and reducing the number of devices on the roads. The principle is applicable to everyone and, even if I use a car company to explain it, also applies to you.

Sometimes I sense a dawning acceptance of new modes of thinking in clients, even if only in small groups of contrarians, and a sincere desire to transform. There needs to be a dawning moment when you accept the value to be gained from addressing vulnerabilities and opportunities arising from unforeseen places in your world.

The eureka moment will be when you experience success and loyalty from collaborating in teams to decide on principles and the bigger purpose you attach to, to help you to win new markets.

Businesses can and will grasp the ideals, principles and core values upon which they can differentiate, and then champion those even more firmly than features and functions they've become over-reliant on.

Those businesses may yet claim their place at the top of customer segments that are choosing to award loyalty to those who share their principles. The sooner one acts the better, because that podium doesn't change hands often.

In summary, the solutions we fixate on can become a limitation when opportunities change in nature. You and your people might be the business's worst enemies if you take into consideration that the nature of needs changes far quicker than humans can anticipate, especially when people operate within a static mindset serving only the as-is way of working.

When the time comes that a lead team decides to diversify, change direction or launch new CTMs, that is when conventional thinking, bound within the outlook of the status quo, is the greatest risk of all. This regularly causes costly misfires, even risking business continuity if enough investment is misplaced.

Embracing the outliers and encouraging collaboration across your business ecosystem is fundamental to succeeding. Success comes from using the insights gained from that inclusive collaboration, within a strategic framework that continuously evolves company strategy and drives action from insights.

Even those ideas that will one day become the new norm for everyone can be fiercely resisted at first. Leaders of these movements need to be courageous and resilient and must have empathy for those they're bringing along with them.

The trick to being more valuable as a business is to solve more customer and partner vulnerabilities and opportunities, further into extended ecosystems. You will need to sharpen your techniques to draw these ideas from within teams, because, for a long period, people will have been subject to continuous reinforcement of conventional thinking attached to the as-is positioning and propositions.

Only by overcoming these limiting factors will you reach the enlightenment moment where the true value opportunities are revealed. Horizons models can provide a safe and comfortable framework for thinking that allows people to direct energy and creativity. This must be without the constraints of worrying that something needs to be achievable today. It must unlock imagination but in a controlled way.

7

Limits Of The Known Versus Unlimited Potential

You've read here that it's your responsibility to reframe a new business context to create a new future. There, you and other businesses will serve stakeholders' desires for businesses of greater principles and purpose. This mood is nearing a tipping point that will result in a step change of buying and employment choices, causing disruptive discontinuity. Your biggest problem might be that somehow you imagine you know the right answers. You might not even be asking the right questions.

To improve the quality of ideas, you need to engage others better. You, your people, and your ecosystem already have the 'right ideas'. You need to ask others, because therein lie the answers to where, how and in what timescales you may succeed.

You know what you know, and some of that even you may temporarily forget. Other people around you know things that you don't. Granted, when you know what you need to find out, and who to ask about it, there's a good chance you'll ask them.

This all represents only a tiny fraction of the true scale of knowledge, experience, opinions and insights at your disposal. I'm hoping you will unearth near limitless opportunity, but you need to throw the net wider, find things you didn't foresee becoming known, and gather all the fish.

People naturally limit their thinking to
the reality they're presented with.

As egocentric humans we rarely go in search of sources of unforeseen knowledge, and we love to tell people what we already know. That one-way flow won't replenish your tanks, it will drain them. Admit it. Sometimes new knowledge isn't welcome. It doesn't fit within comfortable mental boxes that took years to construct.

A person is often loath to admit ignorance or reveal the vulnerability that comes with a lack of ideas. Imagine how much time that wastes and the huge potential for lost opportunity. Why would you imagine asking about something that doesn't even appear on your personal radar, and is therefore unforeseeable?

You need to cut out the time lag between the here and now and an unforeseen future state that is, well, unforeseeably better. This could be an insurance broker choosing to perpetuate paper-based admin while cheaper and easier computerisation is available. They lack the capacity to reveal their vulnerability through open enquiry.

What about me, in my business, persisting with receiving email enquiries from my website and manually juggling all that information? Why didn't I discover, through open enquiry, the automation in customer relationship management systems able to transform life for the better?

Everyone is a little guilty of carrying the burden of unhealthy habitual thinking and working patterns and holding these close to their hearts. Sometimes these are acquired through life experiences and form comfort zones we choose to occupy. Often, these unhelpful and costly assumptions are imposed upon us by others in positions of greater ecosystem influence, either for their convenience or their material gain. The latter is comparable to hegemony, which I'll briefly explain.

Let's talk about hegemony

Hegemony is an interesting word, which I learned when coaching my son during his studies in graphic design. One definition I like is that 'Cultural hegemony refers to domination or rule maintained through ideological or cultural means. It is usually achieved through social institutions, which allow those in power to strongly influence the values, norms, ideas, expectations, worldview, and activities of the rest of society.'[25]

People in visual communications are often nonconformists, and their alternative perspective is ideally suited to spot many facets of hegemony affecting us. Sometimes they influence us to see outside the box of hegemony, and other times they establish new forms and reinforce our beliefs in ways that suit selfish aims.

---

25   Cole, 'What is cultural hegemony?'

Advertisers selfishly encode us with a 'need' for consumerist self-gratification; supposedly self-actualisation from acquiring their products. I mockingly describe grand shopping malls as 'the cathedrals of the consumerist religion'. A hegemony exists that compels us, in various ways, to own homes, to become married young, to own an expensive car and to wear branded clothing and accessories.

While you won't like to admit it, in many parts of your life you are an addictive follower of hegemony in some form. The mere fact that you are human is enough for me to know this. To deny it is to deny your humanity. It's a truism beyond dispute. Rather than debate, imagine where you might gain by challenging some redundant assumptions.

If you are to create new norms, you will need a means to challenge these locked-in habitual patterns that limit achievement of potential.

Hegemony reduces your ability to challenge norms where outrageous and unlimited alternatives are required.

Having written what I have, forgive me for being my own contrarian (it's what I do) and saying a little hegemony can be a good thing. Sometimes we do indeed want people to keep their heads down and get on with keeping the machine turning. After all, if everything was unbounded, everything being reimagined, anarchistic in a sense, we might quickly find ourselves in a mess.

A friend of mine operates a recycling centre, employing many operatives who separate plastics from papers and metals. This is vital in waste management. While there's little true global impact, at least it reinforces environmental awareness and repurposes a fraction of these materials. It's a worthwhile start.

His staff are convinced their role is making an impact on saving the planet. Consider the consequences of enlightening those operatives about the futility of their efforts. How badly it would harm the system if they knew the output of their labour would soon be in a landfill on a different continent or burned and releasing toxins breathed by villagers in far-off countries. Releasing them from their hegemony might send those vital workers off to become activists or demoralise them into reduced productivity. Maintaining their beliefs could be the right way, at least for now.

Harmfully holding onto entrenched thinking and
beliefs traps you in a corner with no way out.

You cannot afford to become so locked into a paradigm that you fail to chart a safe course for your company. Michael Porter created the Five Forces Model I introduced in Chapter 4 to provoke us to consider all aspects of market forces that can affect a business. Thinking ahead, you would build up a brick wall in the path of competitors who would crash into it as they tried to catch you. Sadly, when stuck in rigid habitual thinking, it's likely you will one day see a brick wall someone else built in your path.

It's not just about watching fearfully for the
surprise moves of others. You can become
the disruptor they fear.

We all know business equivalents of the dodo that I described in Chapter 1. You may remember that the dodo moved from being at the top of the food chain to extinction within a century due to the unforeseen arrival of a new entrant in that ecosystem – humans. There are so many examples of businesses also guilty of ignoring threats and failing as a result.

Old-town US mom-and-pop general stores and British high-street shops are failing in their steadfast resistance to oppose the shift to edge-of-town strip malls and superstores. Unless they do something about it, there is little difference between their dogmatic entrenched thinking and that of the dodo.

I was surprised to hear that Blockbuster did not simply fall victim to the 'surprise' emergence of cheaper and better online streaming alternatives. I have been told by a reliable source that they had in fact already negotiated one of the first options to acquire Netflix at a bargain price. That would have been the triumph of that decade. The biggest surprise was that they then reversed that plan, opting to remain bricks and mortar instead. Entrenched thinking won, or for a short time it seemed so.

The question is whether you are limiting your thinking to the reality you are presented with, that could have been thrust upon you by outside forces; whether you have formed those beliefs and assembled them to create a box for yourself that seems safe, warm and easier to manage, at least for the time being.

Permission to imagine and reveal ideas

The Five Horizons Model represents a clean way of planning in relatable time slots. By creating a safe space and inviting people to join you for a time-limited journey through time and value chains, you can free people to imagine how your future will unfold. Reaching across interlocking dimensions of value chains, you can find new places to add value.

You only need decide the time frames, in broad ranges of months or years, and the boundaries where you can influence value or impact. Once you open yourself and facilitate the openness of those you invite into that safe space with you, the ideas will flow.

Decide if you'll be a teller or a listener.

As a young man, I was hungry to learn about how 'real leaders' made strategic decisions. Granted, this was a long time ago, and the lessons I was offered were symptomatic of the time. Then, leaders felt they should tell and others should comply. It is illuminating to consider this attitude and whether it persists.

The 'self-appointed thought leader' I asked spoke firmly about the need to decide on the right answer before consulting 'people lower down', to give them a feeling that they are contributing. One should, I was told, guide the answers they provide so it leads them to validate the decision you had predetermined. The lesson was that the mediocre intellects in your team might believe they shaped the decision. With a smile he explained how he skilfully made them feel that way. Honestly? Machiavelli must have been smiling in his grave.

Perhaps you know someone like this. A boss maybe. It was a great learning moment, though. In hindsight, this was one of the last of the baby boomers a few years older than me, talking to someone from Gen X as though we shared common world views. We were in totally different universes.

Even then, as a younger junior person, I knew intuitively that this man was weak. He lacked the character to reveal himself as knowing less than his team. He didn't understand the idea that Dale Carnegie had been reiterating since the 1930s: one of the most powerful human urges is a thirst to be valued.[26]

In contrast, I've only ever gained respect and loyalty, and new, better ideas, by admitting to teams I need to know what they know, because I only know what I already know. I rely on this to achieve my success.

Overcome the general preoccupation with metrics and free people from self-imposed limited thinking.

Performance metrics relate better to the previous Horizon 0 than they do to the emerging future. That's normal and perhaps appropriate. Nobody will accuse you of being short-sighted by keeping people focused on those metrics.

No industry, no business on this planet, can be assured everything will remain the same. Perhaps not even all the way through Horizon 1. Every situation existing right now will be experiencing

---

26 Carnegie, *How to Win Friends and Influence People*

some level of disruption. That will be in one of the five forces, somewhere in the interconnected chain of value chains, and sometime in the time horizons that lie in front of you.

Like stone being chiselled from the base of a cliff under your feet, your market is changing as you rest. If that change takes you by surprise, it'll be due to your inability, or unwillingness, to step out of the current Horizon 1 metrics and thinking.

The US east-coast leadership of one of the largest global software companies asked me to lead a turnaround of their small services business. In a compressed timescale, drastic revenue losses seemed impossible to reverse. Mid-level leadership resisted.

I knew they would grow product sales far quicker with a services-led value proposition. Three key choices resulted in a successful 100% growth within six months. This is how their leadership discovered they had no choice but to open themselves to change and, in doing so, succeeded.

Firstly, the leadership team agreed to a bold new ambition. Initially digging their heels in and insisting that a 15% growth target would be a stretch, they reluctantly reached a consensus that 100% growth was necessary and realistic.

Secondly, a project of simplification was needed. The business had been hindered by a ninety-six-step legal and administrative process. The smaller simple contracts could easily be expedited at much lower cost and time overheads.

Finally, disjointed product-focused specialists struggled through siloed short-termism. Shifting into collective thinking mode helped them to ignore their product-performance metrics. Their ambition grew and they learned to reinvent customer-focused propositions of far broader scope and greater business value impact.

All of this was achieved by a team that did not believe in its own future. Taking them on a few time-limited journeys through time and value chain space, they visualised, manifested and delivered a great new reality for themselves.

You have limitations too. Imagining on your own limits ideas and builds obstacles.

After reading *War and Peace* by Leo Tolstoy, I had an epiphany. Leaders and followers alike suffer from a grand delusion that great movements of people in history are caused by the genius and prowess of great leaders. It is a fallacy, and that falsehood leads to unhelpful assumptions at every level of society.

History and events of the day are shaped by the ideas or opinions within cultural movements that form in societies, markets, teams. This becomes unstoppable when they gather up sufficient mass and momentum that a tipping point is reached.[27]

As I described in the River Thames story in Chapter 3, tidal-like opinion changes are not obvious to onlookers, except for emerging leaders, who tend to spot what is coming and realise when the critical mass is approaching. Leaders arising in those times simply tap into the existing energy of others and get the timing right. Often, their greatest skill is having foresight into the

---

27   Tolstoy, *War and Peace*

changing beliefs that are emerging and becoming pervasive. They then embolden societies to act on them.

Many of history's great leaders did indeed act. They did so by setting appropriate bold plans. Perhaps through sheer self-belief, they persisted single-mindedly when others might have seen sense and stopped sooner, in some cases before millions perished. These bold plans, however, would never have arisen without a premeditation, or at least a propensity, among the masses, those populations who appeared to be following blindly.

With this perspective, one begins to understand that the greatness of strategy might arise from below, not from the top. These leaders are attuned to the mood, discovering emerging and pervasive ideas that exist within their society, community or company. It's this skill you need, and you need a discipline and structure for that. This will not be achieved by imagining and creating in isolation then attempting to convince the masses afterwards. That's the style that the thought leader I described earlier would have led me to believe was the best.

The human need to be valued is the most powerful energy to leverage.

As referred to previously in the teachings of Dale Carnegie, we all share a deeply held human need to be valued and appreciated. Inclusiveness, therefore, is not just a word that you include in your list of company values on a website and imagine that's the job done.

If inclusiveness is genuinely your intention, you might just have what it takes to be a great leader. By truly valuing others, you're able to find golden nuggets that could help you predict the future beyond the metrics of Horizon 1. Those golden nuggets are quite likely to exist in the minds of people you need to treat with inclusiveness.

When I heard Mindy Gibbins-Klein's message, it resonated firmly with me. She spoke of how we achieve thought leadership through inclusive 'thoughtful leadership'. Mindy insists that one's ego needs to be left outside the door and we should avoid referring to ourselves as thought leaders. Counterintuitive, you might think. Sensible if you aim to build company-level leadership. Ask yourself if you accept that the greatest source of potential thought leadership can be derived from others around you. If you answer yes, the notion of thought leadership becomes collective rather than individualistic.[28]

I loved the idea that everyone feels a sense of worth and validation from recognition of the unique value of their ideas. Absorbing those ideas and combining them to a company-level strategic asset complements your business goals and improves your ability to succeed as a respected leader of others.

Do this with genuine intention and openness to learn from others. Face it: boldly thrusting your concrete ideas onto them is the ultimate in self-indulgence and egocentric thinking.

You'll discover that the people you involve in such a journey, who co-create your purpose, will become more devoted to your cause. Far more devotion than you could ever achieve by handling ideation alone.

---

28   Gibbins-Klein, *The Thoughtful Leader*, referenced here with the author's permission

A culture of inclusivity

My experience in telecommunications company transformation processes is that often where they applied the word 'transformation' in titles it was interchangeable with 'rescue' or 'resuscitate'. My coalescence of all these experiences will be represented as a fictitious company in this book, which I will refer to as SimpLeco.

Imagine a transformation aimed to drag the business back from toppling over a precipice. In my story there is a rapidly approaching tipping point likely to cause hundreds of job losses. Aging and increasingly irrelevant ways of working had been left too long without being challenged or course corrected. As always seemed to be the case, I faced an entrenched team of devoted senior employees. To paraphrase Thatcher – the team was not for turning.

There will always be those people who sullenly
pull you towards the precipice.

Please allow me a moment to admit a personal flaw. It is through many trials and a few failings that I've learned to adapt my approach and the advice I offer. Having succeeded in agile and adaptable teams, I once imagined I would achieve similar remarkable results in all cases. I was, of course, quite wrong.

I didn't help myself by denying the inherent limitations of culture. I also assumed too much of the effect my reputation in the industry would have. That would have translated to nothing more than puffed-up ego in the eyes of old-school battle-hardened tribal warriors.

There would be too great a gap for me to straddle unless such a team invented the solution with me. In their experience of corporate change, senior managers pass through en route to their next promotion. The net result was that this team would lack belief in my pitch; lack belief in me. The tangential path I might propose could have realistically created a better future state for them, or at least permitted their survival in the workplace.

I will retell verbatim a most valuable lesson from one respected technically savvy old boy. He killed the initiative with one glance around the room at his colleagues. Nameless here of course, he told me something that I've never forgotten. 'Steve,' he said with a look of concern for me, 'you have to understand I've been here a long, long time. In that time, I've seen ideas come and go. What can I say? The tide, it goes in, and the tide goes out. Nothing here will ever really change.'

Doom would be the alternative they'd rather have embraced. They preferred that than to accept a demonstrably superior strategy offered by a proven formidable authority in such transformations. After a lengthy battle of wills, my contribution did succeed in delaying their demise. Only for a few years. After my departure, many jobs were eventually lost. Perhaps if strategy had been more slowly co-created with them, their belief may have been greater, and that could have improved the outcome.

Even the best inclusiveness slogan
doesn't equate to success.

In one other business that will remain nameless, I was struck by how genuinely the idea of inclusiveness was made part of the fabric of how leaders lead and how teams do teamwork. It was my first experience of such well-executed corporate values. I realised, of course, that this existed not just because of strategy, but because it was in the nature of the people – the nature of those doing the hiring, and the people they hired in their own likeness. Even in the best of businesses, though, things do go wrong.

For inclusiveness to make an impact, one needs to take to heart the opinions of outliers, not just opinions that are aligned to your thinking or the core thinking. That means listening to, and hearing, and absorbing, inputs from everyone in the room. If inclusiveness is only functioning to reinforce the status quo and comfort (danger) zones that have formed, one loses out on the potential. After all, inclusiveness might help to unearth unforeseeable ideas from nonconformists in your midst.

In that business, there was a norm that existed, and rigid obedience to that norm contradicted this culture of inclusiveness. It limited their ability to truly grasp new kinds of opportunities during their transformation, the ones that require new ways of thinking and working. Evolving from a traditional business model, this had imprinted a culture of adherence to process and rigid governance in standard ways of working. I recall smiling at jibes being made at the expense of their emerging consulting business, which was the target of their transformation, because the dogma of bureaucratic standards was irrelevant and impossible to sustain in that agile advisory business.

Strange but true: asking the wrong question
of the wrong people gets bad results.

Their approach taken to transform would be doomed. Like me, you may have seen this before. First, some of the oldest and most trusted people would be appointed to lead a transformation. As though it was a subconscious intention, this approach led to a new way that was only slightly different to their existing norm.

When that inevitably failed to satisfy the need, outsiders would be hired into the firm. Inbound people arrive boasting impressive résumés from working at companies in adjacent sectors. The hope for 'great geniuses' simply doesn't translate to anything of lasting impact. The value offered by these 'new suits' serves to repeat old ideas. That doesn't help because their main weakness is they lack an ability to imagine something fresh that would be suited to the reinvention needed in each firm's context.

There is bound to be a group of outliers in their midst. Whether hired on purpose or simply arriving coincidentally, their experience will be atypical of the firm's norm. In the face of unconventional thinking among such competent and qualified outliers, the power base operating in the core mindset often won't know how to react and seeks to reassert superiority based on seniority.

Such a team would be a fertile place to find the truly tangential ideas required to make that step shift and capture corporate value differently. A culture of inclusivity should enable those responsible to embrace these outliers. They could adapt extraordinarily powerful know-how into the new ways of working. If done well, the firm could move from catch-up mode into a position of leadership. Too often, that doesn't happen.

A form of antibodies will react in a most counter-logical way. The most inclusive of firms I've seen can become exclusive. It seems 'different' is OK, but only so far as it's not 'too different'.

Given a choice between a helpful big change that challenges the embedded precepts, versus a tiny change that reinforces a beloved comfort zone, those inside the core mindset frustratingly prefer the latter. How frequently one can observe this among those who believe that they know best and that others should follow.

Being inclusive, and using that to embrace uncomfortable or unfamiliar ideas, could be exactly what you need. That could be the secret sauce to set yourself up for achievement. Form a purpose and a framework to guide your collaboration.

Encourage individuals into open dialogue. Neither lock in boundaries, nor be boundless. Establishing a commonly accepted purpose is an important step before asking people to share their inner voices in group work. That is best done interactively, with an open mind, with enough ambition, yet also expressed honestly to reveal limitations.

Enough ambition means: if aiming for greatness then the purpose you offer must match that ambition. If lacking this, the chances are people attending that process with you won't be provoked into true thoughtfulness.

Honesty means: if your company is running out of money and needs to achieve several breakthroughs to survive, it is best you face up to it openly. It can only harm confidence in your leadership if you avoid that reality and create an unrealistic hypothetical purpose.

Make a dedicated working session or cluster of sessions to address these concepts. Workshop models exist that I have used to great effect. It's not necessary for me to show slides and wallcharts here for you to grasp the fundamentals of what you need to do. This is about how you take your chosen group through that time-limited journey through time and value chain space.

I described earlier my Five Horizons Model and Porter's Value Chain and Five Forces Model. Imagine you have hung these images on the wall, there to remind people to open their minds. This is for extracting people from the confines of where their day jobs demand their focus and directing them out across the entire ecosystem.

Everything you decide upon for the strategic roadmap needs to be timed and located somewhere on the Five Horizons Model and can be associated with topics in Porter's models.

You need to provide time in your working sessions for participants to occupy different states of mind. The Disney Model suggests using the terms 'Dreamer', 'Realist' and 'Critic'. What's important is how you bring that to life rather than just telling people, 'OK, now we are dreaming' and then, 'Now is our time to be realists.'[29]

You need to lubricate people's minds and enable them to reach a state of flow. To achieve this, first allocate time for the group to be in a state of conformism. Ask them to tell their past story and status quo. Then move into contrarianism, encouraging people to poke holes and challenge assumptions and conformism as vigorously as they can. Ask them to brainstorm optimistically

---

29   UNaLAB, 'Walt Disney method'

about a hypothetical future of exaggerated ambition, and then one filled with catastrophe. Enjoy that process.

Fine-tuning, you and they will reach a consensus on specific plans and tasks. Again, in these processes you need to guide them into the appropriate state of mind. Team commitment to these bold promises is your last step.

You have a choice to ask for unbounded inputs. Or you can delineate and restrict creativity to areas that you deem open to rethinking. You're free to set boundaries and that could be sensible. I'd argue that pre-emptively reducing scope of enquiry shows a lack of confidence in the capacity of others to apply reasonable and relevant creativity. It also reveals a closed-minded outlook on where potential exists for gain, and effectively removes opportunity to learn from outlier opinions.

When people are locked in habitual thinking and working patterns could be when they're least able to provide a nonconformist perspective to achieve breakthrough. Leadership can be a powerful lever to release them from those mental chains, at least for a time-limited strategic discovery.

The simple act of setting a boundary or fixed direction is a choice you need to carefully consider. Decide what you need and then ask for it. If you need to take a tangential pill, then, by limiting scope of enquiry, you are telling people the confines of your openness.

Your true aim could be best served by discovering something you had never imagined, something that could lie outside any frame of reference you can define. Don't just listen to your outliers but do whatever it takes to drag ideas from them. Be decisive over the right choice, then be prepared to change.

You will need to drive your ship full throttle. You also need to pivot when and if the circumstances should require it. If you ask for help to plot a course to new kinds of success, the people you invite should also share ownership of an executable plan. Then you need to accept that even the best of such plans, as soon as it exists, becomes the norm that you will no doubt need to challenge and test for efficacy.

Be decisive yet flexible with adaptive and agile leadership.

A lot of my work is with technology companies. Founders and investor-appointed executive teams. I've observed there how people can form an unhealthy attachment to the original technical or business model ideas. Any solution, or service, around which they've built a box and in which they have a vested interest, can sometimes take priority over common sense. Understanding this risk and mitigating against it is vital.

I mentioned Stephen Chadwick in Chapter 6, who asked for my help when he was CEO of a private-equity-backed data science and machine learning start-up. In the space of a year, he had turned the business on a dime, building upon a core competency he'd found in the machine learning and data science skills of the team. The product was relaunched as a software-as-a-service. The team refocused on large facilities management providers and a proposition co-created with an insurer. Overall, a remarkable turnaround.

The key point about Stephen's leadership style was that, while using the structure of strategic analysis, he opened to every single member of that team and maintained control. They all trusted the strategy and stayed with the business through a sense of belief in their shared goals and commitment. That inclusive style was on show every week, enabling the agility needed and ensuring the team kept the required direction and speed.

To achieve maximum impact on company-level value, my role is never to congratulate leaders for how well they've done. I was there to secure the necessary major wins, to magnify the issues that limited success, and then accelerate transition to the correctly formatted future version of their business. These factors provided the ability to move from growth potential to real performance, improving attractiveness and valuation for potential investment.

This kind of adaptive repositioning might only happen occasionally. Remaining in this state constantly would cause problems. I find that a business usually needs to tackle these issues when approaching one of the major growth inflection points, or at fundraising events, or to gain maximum value pre-exit. Approaching these moments, often the old operating model, people and technology need to be revisited. Especially if growth and increasing company-level value is to continue beyond that point and not plateau.

Inclusive and adaptive systems keep the
desired level of central control.

Though the size of this next example may be irrelevant to you, the challenge they face is the same as the one you will face, if not now, then soon. The company is a small start-up for building digital and user experience solutions. Two years after launch they numbered 200 employees and were still growing. All products they create are for competitive advantage of the parent company and are highly effective.

An example of best practice was their ability, through flat hierarchy, to allow product owners and agile development managers to operate with relative autonomy. Original business cases were shaped with 100% focus on the value impact for end business users. At the kick-off of each six-week sprint, they checked and course corrected focus within the teams. Only high-level steering was sought from the COO and CEO. Communication with business users was constant as they would deliver the valued outcomes using the technology delivered.

With an inclusive system of working like that, a certain level of trust and delegation is needed. In turn, that requires leaders to accept occasional outcomes that might not be precisely what was originally foreseen. This needs to be combined with rigorous standards that everyone agrees to work within, that unleashes potential and protects the business and individuals. Above all, the focus is on increasing beneficial outcomes.

New ideas can become positive enablers.

A lot depends on one's perspective of what 'good' means. Once you decisively settle on a new norm, you need to keep a watchful eye on new ideas. Once you've embraced them, it's those new norms that can soon become problematic.

Sometimes these can be false positives that cause more damage than good. In some cases, stakeholders demand a return to the old way. With your strategic lens, you need the confidence to ascertain whether the new way simply must persist.

Whether you agree or disagree with the vegan movement, it is obvious from looking in shop windows that this has become mainstream. Visit a shoe shop and you will see vegan shoes. Vegans and conscious consumers may assume these are better in every way, and that would presumably be because they are not produced using animal skin.

While this new paradigm somehow takes root, it also needs to be challenged. Although brands are boasting 'vegan', it could be they are doing harm overall. You may be happy to accept that PVC is the best and most sustainable alternative to leather, but PVC and other petrochemical by-products cannot easily be recycled, and probably never will be.

Leaping onto the vegan band wagon, shoe producers have been permitted to disguise what is a crime against the environment as being righteous. I predict that these brands will be called out for their lack of investment in a vegan solution that is environmentally sustainable. That moment could be harmful to their brands.

Conversely, in many areas the public roads are becoming no-go zones for non-residents passing through in their motor vehicles. Even those visiting friends and family are at risk of receiving hefty penalties. This is part of an overall strategy to end our addiction to motor vehicle transport for the shortest journeys. In parallel, local government will partner with industry to provide cargo bikes, e-bikes, electric quads and pay-per-use cars and vans.

There is a growing sense of militant objection from citizens demanding free use of the roads, arguing that this infringement on freedom of movement is unacceptable. Perhaps correctly, the enforcers are likely to persist, because only by doing so will both our physical wellbeing and the environmental good be better served. In the long term, perhaps we should be getting on our bikes and riding there. I suggest that any local official who surrenders to citizen pressure and reverses these plans could be harshly judged in future years.

There are examples of decisiveness that absolutely must be upheld as new norms. There are also examples that might well cause damage soon if not reversed. Be inclusive, watchful, alert to the best ideas, adaptive and forever aware of your impact, both positive and negative.

In summary, established norms and beliefs become habitual and, in business, can cause limitations preventing you from reaching your true potential. The world is filled with such inhibitors to free thought, and you need to become the one who is able to release people from those constraints.

If you're good at this, it may become a tool for you to find ways by which you become that competitor making the unexpected move that confounds others. Valuable techniques have been provided that allow you to take teams into safe zones for the imagination, where you need to perfect the process of listening and resisting the urge to confine their ideas or telling the answer prematurely.

As willing as you may be to open minds to new options, it is a habit of most people to form boxes that confine thinking. Your innovation could rapidly become your new dogma. Somehow, you need the strength of character to empower free expression without running into unbounded chaos. Often the answer lies in knowing when to change and when not to change and that is littered with opportunities to misjudge, considering you are only human. Thinking it through and seeking others to challenge your judgement is often the right approach.

8

Inspired People Think Big And Champion Big Shifts

Inspired people think bigger; they hunger for achievement and could become instruments of your success, in whatever the Great Shift means for your business.

The colleagues, partners, suppliers and others that you want to consult all have their short-term priorities. Somehow, you need to temporarily release them, to facilitate future-gazing. You need these people to dig deep, to find where your actions have greatest impact. Once a strategy is activated, they need to feel motivation, so they perpetuate and amplify positive effects. You need to remove the constraints on what your people imagine are the limits, and overcome the short-term measures preventing people from saving themselves.

Way back in 1986 Tom Peters coined the phrase, 'What gets measured gets done.' This might be new to you, or it could be a long-held understanding. At a critical moment for me, it was a hard lesson when this featured in one of the greatest management challenges I'd faced up to then. Side-stepping the short-term priorities and a preoccupation with metrics can be a tricky thing to achieve.[30]

I witnessed circumstances in a tech firm where this challenge was almost insurmountable. It seemed to be a terrifying prospect for people to change, despite the alternative being failure. To quote Simon Phillips the Change Man, 'It seems there's a lure of the status quo as soon as change gets tough, despite the reality that toughness is the gateway to the unknown positive future.'[31]

The challenge I refer to even caused the creation of an entirely parallel team, and yes, they were given metrics and targets that would drive the new team's activities in new ways. I suppose if you can't beat them, in a good cause you might as well join them.

As you know by now, I tend be that person who guides businesses out of comfort zones, or danger zones as I like to call them. I feel justified driving initiatives that are sometimes tangential to the core. Often people living and working inside the core mindset are necessary instruments of the success I seek. It is difficult to crack that nut.

Let's be clear. These growth or turnaround interventions aim to save jobs and preserve the stability of businesses, yet, even when that's the case, it is difficult to entice people away from their predilection for unhealthy norms. The patterns they follow are embodied in the targets and measures they are attached to, which reinforces their limited outlook.

---

30 Peters et al, *In Search of Excellence*
31 Phillips, 'The change man', quoted with the permission of Simon Phillips, The Change Maker Group

Seeking to prove a business model capable of securing 2,000 new named customers a year was a cornerstone for a profitable future of the business. This required whole business units to change, and each involved convincing tens, even hundreds, of people. Each person would need to make personal choices to work in an entirely new model, unique in the industry.

The direct sales team had already accepted next-year targets for 15% growth. The worry was they could achieve that with a bit of sweat and intellect, which would allow them to ignore our strategy. By heaping on a goal of 200% growth, it became impossible for the teams to achieve targets if they handled it the old way, and they knew it.

I learned the power of the maxim, 'targets drive focus'. It was for people's own good, in the long term. Having freedom to create insurmountable targets could force teams to accept change. Allies in the management team understood that their people's willingness to pivot and put their weight behind new strategy was a strength. Only shocking targets guaranteed this great case study would become a success story.

Stay one step ahead of those who ingeniously manipulate targets.

It amazes me to watch how concentrated and ingenious people become in finding ways of manipulating a measure if it helps avoid personal cost or complexity. Though you can't watch their every move, you do need to be better at controlling outcomes.

You might notice experienced people who tend to ignore business change directives yet still exit a season with the highest commission payments. Sadly, those who willingly ignore metrics to follow a beneficially tangential path will often be financially penalised. This is avoidable of course, if planned. Often it becomes the cause of change failure that was unforeseen at the time of target setting.

As a good example, consider our collective acceptance of the need to solve levels of waste, and how that needs some form of recycling or supply chain transformation. The same can be said for the need to reduce carbon emissions in industrial nations.

Central governments offer a budget to local authorities that is dependent on quotas set to recycle waste. Businesses and nations accept obligations to reduce carbon emissions. All too often this results in waste simply being exported to other, poorer countries where it pollutes their environment, and the trading of carbon emissions levels that exceed targets in exchange for credits available from nations that don't cause emissions.

Trickery? Skulduggery? No, just clever navigation of metrics that has the effect of preventing the transformation of polluting processes. All for the sake of cost avoidance and simplicity. This will come back to haunt those who have perpetuated the harm committed within their ecosystems and value chains.

Your success may depend on being skilful in setting metrics to cause people to stop and change their focus and approach. If so, you need to allow yourself more flexibility to adapt and course-correct once you observe whether targets result in the right effects.

This is vital when fine-tuning metrics so people pursue long-range strategic aims, which is almost certainly something they will try to ignore. To succeed, it is helpful to assure them that supporting your innovations will be a net improvement and won't be to their detriment in months and years to come.

Preparing for future horizons and the art of the possible

If you want people to look beyond multiple value chain horizons, you need to lift their gaze from under the weight of overloaded daily routines. This can be tough.

Consider first how people learn to become good at something, then form habitual routines. They feel safe and secure in the boxes and norms they have created.

Compare that with what happens when people face new challenges they need to solve quickly. The two processes are different, to the extent that each of these circumstances causes different nerve signals for the brain functions needed.

The human being has an innate preference for routine. We become comfortable in our habitual patterns of thought and movement. Our biology and nervous system are hardwired to seek out efficiency which, once proven and repeated, forms into a habit. We prefer that to the creativity demanded by unfamiliar processes.

We are creatures that perpetually feel urged to reinforce easier habits. The comfort we experience once secure in these causes feelings of reluctance to release ourselves from them. That's why they're called 'comfort zones', and I have no problem with comfort zones. At least not until they become weaknesses threatening to cause harm – in other words, danger zones. It is worth remembering this when asking people to ignore habits and to innovate.

Your aim is to inspire people to visualise, innovate and create newness, where doing so is valuable. All people exist in a paradigm of the status quo. As humans, we form habits that enable us to simplify and repeat mental and physical processes, supporting the as-is reality. What you are asking is nothing short of inhuman.

I don't suggest for a moment that people are incapable of departing from habits. Quite the contrary. In fact, humans are ideally equipped for that. What I am making clear is that emotionally, physiologically, mentally, even at the level of the central nervous system and brain functions, you are asking for something counterintuitive.

Add to that the power of the routines people live within; their daily humdrum, if you like to call it that. Our instincts mean people learn to love routines, even if they claim to despise them. You may have spent countless evenings and weekends contemplating this journey. Your people didn't foresee the brainstorming request you're about to launch upon them coming.

A piece of research published in *The Financial Times* confirmed what I'd suspected. The capacity to innovate underpins the ability to make productivity gains in businesses. Almost half of gains were anticipated to depend on the capacity of individuals within businesses to innovate. You have probably seen TED talks or read articles with similar messages, or perhaps you've even observed this directly.

When individuals are asked what prevents them from successfully innovating, four in ten blame excessively heavy process workloads, and nearly the same number explain that business processes prevent them from feeling free and able to innovate.

It seems plausible to conclude that, as businesses scale and form reliable processes, employees become preoccupied with habitual patterns of working and thinking. To survive that scale we overload people to the point of mental saturation. When asked to innovate, those people can experience a negative form of emotional, or perhaps even physical, reaction, as though antibodies counteract even the most compelling justification to change.

That is something you cannot ignore. I've written about inviting people into your time-limited journey into the future. If you hope for them to join you willingly and contribute productively, you first need to understand how to help this condition if it affects them. It could be time to change how you measure success.

I recommend you assume you will soon need to include people inside and connected to your business in open-minded innovative engagement, and to consider whether they can be better prepared for this. That is only possible by changing daily working patterns to instigate collaborative activity in the workplace.

I don't mean scheduling finger-painting sessions weekly, unless you imagine that would help. I do suggest that creativity can be embedded into work time. This can take the form of encouraging people to create ideas for improvement and change, and, when doing that, to cement a culture of open-minded debate.

One senior executive at Digital Equipment Corporation invited all teams to offer ideas for improvement. He promised that they'd be rewarded. He assured those who were successful that their ideas would be replicated quickly and globally. His door was wide open, but he stipulated that he only wanted to hear of a new process innovation if it removed the need for two or three others that already existed.

Simple but inspiring. People gained greater motivation in their humdrum work because they felt empowered to leap out of habitual thinking patterns that resulted in perpetuating the as-is. If you want to ask people to reimagine and believe in great future possibilities, make sure they're not blinded by today's reality. Opening minds precedes opening eyes.

I've raised three sons. I've also managed many people in the workplace. Together, these experiences enabled me to draw parallels and form insights which I will describe, as they provided me with valuable lessons.

I always take care to ensure I am present and involved throughout. I was a present father, just as I was a present manager. I'm sure this sometimes caused some annoyance, and perhaps my occasional absence might have been preferred.

From micromanager to coach

My partner and I needed to spoon-feed our sons in every sense when they were babies, let's say fresh-faced innocent new recruits. Babies don't know what they don't know. As toddlers, finding their feet and early independence, without us spelling out the dos and don'ts they might never have learned to improve valuable formal and informal skills.

Using a workplace parallel, parents need to be like micromanagers. All parents and managers reach a stage when their subjects change suddenly. With age and experience, parents should then become manager-delegators. Successful people adapt habitual patterns from being like 'tell-mode' managers to becoming a coach. As every businessperson knows, the subtleties of that change elude many.

Part of the illusion of the 'manager-mode' addiction is to believe we cause others to act, or to assume it is possible to create motivation in another person. For instance, leaning over a person and telling them to study or work, parents or managers watching each step and telling their children or team what to do next. It's unhealthy and it fails to develop either person, or to strengthen the relationship between them.

The single greatest gift I gave to my children and to my team members was to insist that they needed to find their own motivation. It took time, and along the way there were many moments when I teetered on the edge of panic that they would never find their personal vision or self-motivation.

I just tried to be the best coach that I could, failing occasionally. I only stepped back into micromanaging when they proved to be a danger to their own success. This coaching style left no alternative but for my children and my team to realise they were the captains of their own future, not me. When faced with a real opportunity to fail, they chose success.

Part of this process was to try to help them visualise that their present reality was not representative of the future they could experience. In the confines of the secondary school sausage-machine education system, having a vision for the future was difficult. Employees feel the same, pressured under the burden of a daily workload and mental challenges. In both situations, that made it difficult to see there would ever be a changed reality. Only when they saw through the haze and visualised something better did I see a spark of self-motivation ignite.

Allowing people to remain fixated, with a limited view of only their business-as-usual in Horizon 1, will limit their belief in a better future. It is your task, as their leader, to present a glimpse at future horizons. Giving them a hand in shaping and manifesting that future reality motivates creativity and gains their involvement.

Don't suppose that you can predict the opinions you'll discover when you're trusted with them.

I have found various means to establish trust with people in my teams at work. It often boiled down to showing a genuine interest and empathy with their values and opinions. Yes − surprise, surprise − it helped when I gave credit for their contribution to our successes. Vital in all cases has been my willingness to allow conversations to take me to places that I had not planned for. That was largely achieved by respecting the opinions and values of the other person as much as I did my own.

You might claim this is easy when dealing with mature adults who are employees, so yet again I will return to my parenthood case study. Nobody in their right mind would claim that it's simple to achieve this when negotiating the irrationality of youth, especially when dealing with people who we care for so deeply.

It takes dedicated time and openness to achieve trust, and to be given a licence to offer advice. I spent twenty-four years figuring out my one son's nuanced strengths and limitations. I guided him and supported his six-year visual communication education. We shared joy as he secured a role in design and videography, in what would be an award-winning agency team. I figured that he and I had done a good-enough job.

Similarly, I supported a graduate mentee who was introduced via the Migrant Leaders charity where I sit on the advisory board. I imagined that, once he successfully entered a Big Four firm, he would settle into a rhythm and see through the next few years growing steadily.

My lesson from both cases is that one should be prepared to be surprised as a mentor. I also learned to rely on mentees to show me what's really going on in the world, or in the culture of a business. The chemistry of mutual respect and trust depends on many variables and experiences, accumulated over time, that form into a bond. That trust requires one to discover and accept their nonconformism, too.

I was surprised, and a little disappointed, I'll admit, when my son opened up to me that he was considering going off at a tangent to change his career – into policing. In his case, he hungered for purpose and meaning, much like most of his generation will soon reflect. He would willingly take a lower salary to escape what he called a 'meaningless purposeless existence' working in his company to enrich faceless owners who failed to create a sense of greater purpose that would inspire young staff.

Surely companies can do better than the situation he described. They can form a shared meaning that appeals to this generation's values and gives recognition where due.

My mentee who had recently joined the Big Four firm hungered to realise his potential value and ambitions. Despite the résumé kudos of working there, he was soon considering opportunities elsewhere. The firm had also neglected to respect the individual's readiness and maturity, assuming his willingness to simmer in the soup for two years before any genuine development. He was attracted to a role as business manager to a chief executive in a major telecommunications company. His self-assured decisiveness exemplified Gen Z, which is unlike what I remember from previous generations. No company should assume they are entitled to expect years of a person's energy in exchange for a salary and a desk.

In both cases, I offered words of wisdom in restraint, but I did not resist. By that stage, I was dealing with equals. In respect for their qualities, I supported the tangential paths that each now considered. It would have been easy for me to react badly, to narrow my thinking and refute the value of these tangential ideas. In doing so, I would be ruining all the positivity that had built up in those trusted relationships.

The power of unexpected nonconformism

No matter how unexpected the outcome might be, nonconformist ideas could lead to the best possible result. This is especially attractive when inviting others into a time-limited journey through time with you to visualise a tangential future.

I learned that I am seldom the person who knows all the right answers. Those right answers exist, potentially, somewhere between imaginations in the minds of others around me. If I trust them and allow that potentiality to take shape, I find gold.

I have no doubt that my son and my mentee are correct in their choices, and that their futures will be golden. Just maybe not how I'd anticipated it would be. That's OK. How true that can be in business, too.

Without a shadow of doubt, I can say that these decisions are typical of their generation. My son feels a burning need to have a purpose in life, not simply to enrich people who don't share his principles. He and my mentee both expect and deserve greater personal credit and reward for the value they provide. When valuable but undervalued employees choose to jump ship and change companies, it will be a consequence of companies failing to inspire or reward their young people.

My experience was marvellous. It reminds me how great it feels to just let go, empower people and wait to be amazed or disappointed. Many parallels exist in professional contexts and this approach is a far more powerful mode of leading, as opposed to the loss of talent you will endure if you fail to inspire and reward.

Ask why, and why again, to discover together the 'why' that matters the most. Keep a reality check, and make sure you genuinely affect that outcome.

Even the greatest ideas need to make an impact. You can settle on articulating a minor impact or you can persevere to dig deeper to find a greater impact. Choose to do the latter.

I know a community in the fashion industry committed to sharing best practices and opportunities for sector development in their home country. The message in recent emails has focused on educating on the culpability of the fashion industry in emitting greenhouse gases, up to 10% of the world's total, and on encouraging businesses to differentiate by limiting their effects at the levels of manufacturing, transport of raw materials and finished goods around the world. In other words, keeping their value chain as close as possible to the point of consumption.

I include this as an example of the point I'm making here. It is relatively easy to stay focused on the immediately obvious value outcome. In this case, that the country's fashion businesses deserve to succeed and should work towards that goal. Digging a little deeper, the brand has attached itself to a far greater, globally significant purpose for impact and outcomes.

By doing so, the company has captured the attention of people who share these principles. Perhaps they haven't yet chosen to change suppliers. Once a sustainable alternative is presented, in the context of this campaign of education, they could choose to change suppliers and perhaps even reframe their company value proposition. This would be based on principles they consider important.

Although I've already discussed it at length, it's worth reminding you that Millennials and Gen Z will soon be aged between twenty and fifty. Along the pattern established by Gen X, 72% of them may change suppliers to those who emerge with principles that match their own. Their choices of employers will follow that principles-led model, too.

In this case, the message is realistic. The claim is robust that these outcomes could result from producing fashion ethically with sustainable materials sourced locally. This is a valid statement of purpose linked to an outcome directly affected by the publicist.

Other cases represent exaggeration, misleading the public or customers by greenwashing marketing communications with false claims of making a global impact.

I encourage you to dig deep. Grant your team a licence to imagine where positive impact outcomes can be realistically attributed to your business. While doing that, keep it real. Avoid the risk of exaggeration slipping in that could damage your brand.

A series of interlocked causes and effects
leads to purpose and motivation.

Doing this well can have a rapid and materially significant effect on performance, which has an impact on the general sense of motivation your business can inspire externally. This is best described through a real example.

An ex-employee approached my team for help motivating a large telco to partner with his firm. Technically, their products were suitable. He exaggerated by claiming they were 'amazing'. Clearly this man felt passionately that a partnership should be pushing this into hospitals globally. Somehow, despite feelings that the value should be obvious, he was failing.

Their devices could be worn on a lanyard around the neck, and had all the functionality of a paging device, locator beacon and communicator. Once configured, any member of hospital staff could be geolocated so that, if located near a need they qualified to assist, they would be paged. Within seconds, they'd be communicating verbally, if necessary.

Considering the features, the motivation to buy was low. Despite there being a statistical prediction of convenience and timesaving, and the appeal it held for those who aimed to improve effectiveness of patient care, safety and cost-savings, it seemed likely hospitals would continue using mobile telephones. The only hope was that somehow this technical solution could deliver greater impact in areas of known urgency.

What I'm about to describe is not one of life's great strokes of genius. In fact, it struck me as a somewhat obvious thought process – so much so that I brought a small group together to explore and develop this thinking, feeling certain there must be more to this than my snap judgement. Most remarkable is that nobody at the vendor had been through this thought process until my team prompted it.

I felt genuinely embarrassed that we were praised for ideas that should have been obvious to anyone studying this challenge. It shocked me that this was considered a breakthrough. It went something like this.

My ex-employee was asked, 'Why is it better for people to use your device rather than mobile phones and lists of numbers?' The answer, 'Quicker access to the people who are qualified for a situation and who are located closest to it.'

Then, 'Give me a couple of examples you think would be most valuable.' The answer, 'There are several, but one is to locate a porter and have patients moved more quickly. That would reduce delays in surgery and free up clinical staff to their duties.'

Our response, 'That sounds like an interesting operational improvement. What about something that can save lives?', half expecting he might laugh it off. His answer, 'Well, that's obviously when a crash alarm requires a qualified clinician to respond and resuscitate a dying patient. At present there's no way of knowing which clinician is located closest to incidents; there's no way of alerting the right person to go quickly enough to save the life.'

I cleared my throat. I distinctly remember the pause, and then asking, 'So you mean to tell me that your technology saves lives?' The answer, after hesitation, and a few moments' thought, 'Well… I suppose yes, it does save lives.'

I am a big fan of allowing a few moments of silence for a person's mind to process what they've just declared. Especially when it's that momentous.

We facilitated agreement on a partnering workshare and product mix to motivate the two parties. A joint briefing was circulated to his executives who had their hands on the purse strings. This became a go-to-market partnership, to promote lifesaving and cost-busting technology in hospitals.

Preparing evidence to prove the promised benefits, the argument was easily won. Hospital staff told us they struggled daily with these life-and-death situations, or else with the impossibility of finding a porter when you need one.

We started by asking a few suitable 'why, why, why' questions. The result translated a product which had helpful but uninspiring features into a most compelling new proposition.

I encourage you to work with your chosen team looking into future time horizons. Seek out vulnerabilities and opportunities across the Five Horizons of interconnected ecosystem value chains. Consider all the five forces affecting your market. Challenge your effects for the greatest level of impact you can reasonably claim. Aim to inspire with impact-led and purposeful vision.

People who help shape such purpose and vision will tell others about it far and wide. They will also seek out more ways to win. It makes no sense to be the only evangelist of a vision that you create in isolation. Spend a little time, be inclusive and gain a multiplier effect in a team of evangelists.

Setting aside religious connotations, the origin of the word 'evangelist' is Greek. It meant 'spread the good word'. For four years in the 1980s Guy Kawasaki was Apple's chief evangelist. Jeff Barr has more lately been in that role for Amazon Web Services. Both are in technology companies so forgive me for appearing to have industry bias. The main point of the role implies that a business finds a message, a difference or form of beneficial impact, and evangelists promote that. You can, too.

Use smart Alecs to your advantage

I referred earlier to an old-school war horse who singlehandedly stalled my hypothetical growth initiative in a hypothetical telco we're calling SimpLeco. A single negative glance at colleagues caused that. He was the smart man who said, 'the tide goes out and the tide comes in' and so on. For anonymity, let's call him Alec. Smart Alec.

I wouldn't hold anything against Alec. Alecs in the mix are often smart, and that cleverness becomes useful. After all, maybe it would be correct that any such forthright claim that early ideas are the best solution could be poorly conceived. Who knows? What I can say is that the Alecs in my life have become a great asset.

Examining past success stories, I realise that end customers often don't buy into new ideas because of the SimpLecos of this world. They buy into them after checking with an Alec. When a SimpLeco promises something, customers ask Alec and then decide. If Alec promises something, then customers tend to believe him.

Every business has a useful smart Alec, and maybe several. Use them well.

It's taken me around eighteen months to convince a typical Alec that any of my new ideas were supportable. Somewhere along that timeline, Alec embraces the concept and the working model I propose. We then agree it could be the platform for future success. I've seen one such Alec become an effective evangelist and, in that role for over ten years, the new model we created together succeeded in roughly 95% of customers.

You can make small mistakes. Never, ever forget to include your Alec in the process of time travelling and vision building. You'll never regret any slight inconvenience you experience while convincing your Alec, because they become the best evangelists.

Embedding a sense of belief can be a powerful weapon.

Ask yourself how you create a sense of belief in others. Imagine a group of individuals with varying motives and opinions, different viewpoints of the business and of you. Perhaps they work in different teams or even different companies, with different metrics.

Think back all the way to 1983. That was before the World Wide Web was even a twinkle in the eye of Tim Berners-Lee. Coincidentally, ARPANET, an arm of the US Defence Department, had just started using the Internet protocol suite commonly known as TCP/IP. In 1983, if people wanted to have knowledge at their fingertips, they needed to spend an unholy amount of money acquiring thirty volumes of encyclopaedia.

I remember a story from a reliable source who was then the sales director of an encyclopaedia distributor in South Africa. When training door-to-door salespeople, a well-trodden sales pitch was typically learned parrot-fashion. These hungry foot soldiers would then be unleashed onto the unsuspecting public. Some sales candidates proved more difficult to convince than others, and one stood out as a case study.

A lady in her mid-twenties struggled to accept the training. Having empathy, she was uncomfortable taking money from families, especially such a price for a set of books. They recalled losing patience with her. Taking her to one side, in a quiet but firm tone they confided something in her secretively, almost in a theatrical way.

They explained the 'truth', which was a burden that all their most successful people must understand. That is that these families *need* the encyclopaedias if their children are to have any chance of being successful at school or university. The emphasis was that she, and only she, would be able to save these families. Otherwise, imagine the torment and disappointment of seeing their children struggle unnecessarily. The only possible way of them helping their children to succeed was to sign and buy.

She became quiet and contemplative. The sales director suspected he'd lost her and returned to the training room to continue with other candidates. She returned after twenty minutes with a focus that was almost unnerving. She was transfixed on every tiny detail and had energy at a level that surprised everyone there.

The nature of that breed of salesperson was crude. Pretty much like the worst of the Apprentice sycophants of Donald Trump or Alan Sugar. The director was terribly proud of the pet sales-monster he had created. For several months, the lady had achieved the highest sales results of her cohort, earning quite a large commission.

They chuckled, recalling how she was driven by simple-minded belief in the 'lines' they had fed to her. She had relentlessly pursued and harassed families until they surrendered and 'did the right thing for their young children'. An added unexpected bonus was her success selling additional regular updates of volumes. I have no doubt that the true values of that encyclopaedia company were not reflected in their distributors' style of selling, but that is, after all, one of the effects of the principle, 'What you measure and reward is what you should expect to get.'

It seems that, in her euphoric state of belief and motivation, this salesperson sought out more and more ways to help deliver the impact she had now embraced as her purpose.

I always feel uncomfortable retelling that story to people. This crass form of pushy selling is against my personal preference. I do not want to create an impression that I support or associate myself with such practices. I retell this just to illustrate the power of creating evangelists. This can be based on belief and a sense of purpose, and the rewards one can gain from that are surprisingly great.

Think of any salesperson who is that passionate and inspired, believing in beneficial outcomes they can deliver to customers. Then add to that by enlightening them with the knowledge that this aligns with their personal principles. You'll find that they will naturally tell more people and find new ways to deliver impact or outcomes to ever greater levels than first envisioned.

In summary, the key impacts you can directly affect should be uncovered together with those people who could be priceless evangelists delivering your beliefs in every aspect of your value chain. The better your business embodies that purpose and principles-led positioning, the more potent your differentiation may become.

There are techniques you need to learn that allow you to relieve people from metric-led and process-dominated lives, so they might help with precision and insight. It's up to you to adapt to those insights in ways that enable people to apply their collective energy to your success. Don't underestimate the inertia and resistance caused by ignoring this. People could even become instrumental in their own failure if it makes them feel more comfortable to remain in current modes of working and thinking. You need to be their enabler.

Nonconformism and outlier opinions can be your friend, and willingness to trust and be trusted allows you a chance to find where the greatest value exists in those sources. Among these sources of insight, you can find the most remarkable forms of impact your business can lay claim to, which offers a surprisingly potent competitive advantage when you select wisely and act decisively.

These might not yet be at the front of your mind, and, in fact, they will probably be unforeseen. When you boil it back to basics it is likely that, after educating markets that competitors lack or ignore these critical principles or values, your positioning can cause customers to change.

9

Challenge For Gaps And New Ideas

After perhaps a lifetime of seeking to feel assured you've got things right, it may feel counterintuitive to ask others now to challenge your ideas. On the other hand, making a habit of asking for constructive criticism is how you improve.

You need to find a positive approach to question your assumptions of what's good enough. My apologies in advance, to perfectionists or self-doubters, for whom it can feel relieving or triumphant finding a rhythm of 'all is well'. Respectfully, I ask you to leave that behind and take a path that will seek contradiction, deconstruct assumptions and rebuild.

Showing your willingness to accept this, even to promote contradiction, could become a great strength. Create a systemic norm of doing this in search of the best forms of innovation. That could already be present nearby without you knowing it.

Define your model for self-challenge.

It is helpful to define your own model. Set this into the rhythm of your work to seek out weaknesses, gaps and opportunities. Your task is then to use that ammunition to find ways to inform strategy, to align execution behind those insights.

The pandemic of 2020 caused more widespread and greater intensity of isolation than we've ever seen before. Isolated lifestyles had been apparent before then, but it all came into sharper focus in a new reality of forced lockdown and online meetings. Because, as humans, we tend to think in isolation and, above all else, we value our own conclusions, this worsened existing poor communication habits and weakened an already flawed tendency not to evolve through listening to others.

Over several decades, long before social media or mobile phone texting, we saw communication styles worsening. That is not a technology-driven phenomenon, but a human weakness amplified later by technology. I recall listening to Steven Covey talk about relearning how to communicate with his son, to stop talking at him to reach a predetermined answer.[32] This is nothing new.

This was all brought into sharp focus when on several occasions I heard complaints about 'unintelligent conversation'. The general impression is that people don't ask each other open questions when conversing; they just speak, and mostly about the stuff that they already know about, showing no interest in what others might know about a subject.

---

32   See, for example, Covey, *The 7 Habits of Highly Effective People*

This appears to be part of the human condition. The sensory experiences our brains process are all subject to our thoughts. We live within our minds to form opinions and draw conclusions, and all this in isolation. The more isolated we are, the less we ask others to help us, and the more stuck we become in our viewpoints. It seems like we value our own intellect above that of others.

This pattern of assuming the correctness of one's own conclusions isn't surprising. As a result, it becomes counterintuitive to ask others, but that doesn't make it right. Needing to claim you're the best, and have the answers, can become addictive. I'm highlighting this tendency so you can avoid it, proactively and systematically.

It is good to have belief in your product and company, and in yourself of course. Yes, outwardly show absolute confidence your 'stuff' is the best. For the sake of strategic effectiveness, you should also ask, 'What if it isn't the best?' Surely, if it's not, then isn't it better to face the facts, course-correct or just do something different? At the least, stop believing in some fictitious differentiation that exists only in your mind.

Failure to self-challenge means you could form false illusions of superiority, and that leads only in one direction. Failure. You might believe in such ideas, but sooner or later employees and customers will see through them. Take a reality check. Asking for honesty from others can become your salvation.

In over 200 strategic client workshops, participants consistently exaggerated the positive in blind assumption of competitive superiority. True, that is occasionally possible, but not in every company and for most of their products, which is pretty much what I was being asked to believe.

As a leader, yes, you want your people to feel they represent the best, even if your market's overcrowded. You, however, cannot afford to be blindsided by wishful thinking. Tip: you cannot win the grand prix in a family car just because you boast to neighbours it's high-performance. Be honest with yourself. Express a willingness to be contradicted, then ask others to do the same.

Nonconformism and contrarianism are often-misunderstood virtues. It is important to understand the intention of a contrarian, rather than to automatically accept or dismiss them. It's also important to be clear about your own purpose, if this is the role and approach you choose to take on.

A positive definition, relating to investors, describes a contrarian as a person who 'makes decisions that contradict prevailing wisdom'. That person has potential, perhaps to avoid the perils of groupthink based on outmoded thinking.

Another definition reveals the most popular negative perception, describing 'a contrary or obstinate person'.[33] It's not unusual for groups to gang up against someone who dares to contradict an accepted norm.

We've reached a point where dissent from groupthink is discouraged, even labelled as 'obstinate'.

No, you won't get invited to parties if you constantly oppose others and cleverly justify your opposition. Perpetual challenging

---

33   'Contrarian', definition in *The Free Dictionary*

and rethinking norms can cause any consensus to be scuppered as a contrarian shakes it up yet again. There are limits beyond which even good medicine can be poisonous.

That's outweighed by the damage caused by being unwilling to allow healthy challenge of assumptions and accepted norms. One entrepreneur I know has banned staff from unquestionably agreeing with him. His view is he wastes their experience and intellect unless they're free to think and challenge.

In search of enlightenment

Plenty of references have been made to Einstein's dislike of peer reviews. His view stemmed from his desire for freedom to speculate without critique, and all speculative theories were dismissed in the scientific journals of his time. Except for once-in-a-generation geniuses, which you or I cannot lay claim to be, there is no excuse to avoid critique if we hope to find our A-Game.[34]

The US Constitution wasn't immediately a success. In its original flawed form as Articles of Confederation, it lasted only a few years. The success of the final document was due to the willingness of established leaders to collaborate in a team of fifty-five people to rewrite the Constitution. Some were complete strangers to each other. Without willingness for challenge, and openness to contrarians, such a long-lasting consensus might never have been reached.

After the UK voted to leave the EU, British politics kicked into an overdrive of debate and contrarianism. Those in power

---

34   Marks, 'Einstein's only rejected paper'

couldn't force poorly conceived laws through a parliament that was empowered and obliged to challenge them. Under autocratic regimes, people viewed the British system as an exemplar of fair governance. Yet when the lengthy Brexit debates hit stalemate, that same system was mocked.

It is unfortunate the world perceived that as weakness and a chaotic lack of leadership. I viewed it differently. That feature of British democracy which prevents autocracy is a strength.

The public worldwide squirmed when watching the awkward reality of how contrarianism looks when viewed up close and personal. It's neither pretty nor swift. Often, you're forced to hear strange outlier opinions. In such a system there will never be a great leader demanding hundreds of others to 'just do as you're told'.

This is much more effective, even if a little less efficient; it is a strength, not a weakness. Hard-coded openness to accept challenge and contrarianism protects liberty and forces the highest standards possible from leaders, and that includes some who'd prefer to be autocratic. I argue that companies benefit in the same way when openness becomes embedded.

There are plenty of examples in our world today of great or ignoble leaders, of one or the other ideology, or of entrepreneurs who have become dogmatic in their viewpoint. They use any opportunity to act alone to force damaging policies that nobody dares debate. I am pleased to live in a true democracy, and I am proud to have worked in companies with liberal democratic values. Even when that looks a little indecisive, it is for the better.

Look nearby to find ideas, know-how
and differentiation potential. Sometimes a
'grand plan' is proven less valid when
compared to the ingenuity of others.

You will be surprised at the magnitude of cleverness available to you. If you imagine you're the only one solving a problem or capturing an opportunity, chances are you're mistaken.

Accept you might find a better answer from someone else. Finding it then acting upon it is likely to be the most effective route to success. This is an acid test of your inclusiveness, and the best way of proving the true worth of your ideas.

I led a corporate professional community of 2,000 in sales and sales management. It aimed to identify, co-create and make new norms from high-performance best practices. Aspects I imagined would be straightforward turned out to be the opposite.

Settling on critical improvement goals, we identified a best practice for each that stood out, aiming to make it ready to be replicated. In consultation to refine, invariably several pockets of innovation were already solving these elsewhere. Sometimes their solutions were better, even if only in small parts.

Tough choice. Going for efficiency-first meant forcing a standard that could suppress innovators contradicting us. For the long-term win, combining all strengths into one would gain consensus to form the best new norm. The first could be expedited with risks, and the latter would cost us time for the appearance of greater excellence.

I won't tell you the right answer for your circumstances. That would be impossible. If the truth be known, I chose different responses for a wide variety of situations. Sometimes the win was worth slowing down for refinement. Otherwise, time-to-market was a priority, and we sacrificed goodwill for that.

You might imagine you have the best answer. Chances are many imagine the same of themselves and could deeply resist. Whether or not they are correct, they have a viewpoint.

You gain more by being inclusive and effective,
rather than being autocratic and efficient.

Reinventing to accelerate

Especially in large companies spread across country operations, but also in small groups of people, there are important decision-making hierarchies. Chapter 1 showed slowness in accepting new ideas among stakeholders even when mitigating threats from industry disruptions.

Internal hierarchies built for traditional product launches can become resisters when innovations are proposed. This natural antibody protects from harmful distraction. In digital disruptions, burdensome decision-making can kill a company. You will find that pertinent in your customers' decision-making, too.

I recommend that in these circumstances companies create vastly different models. Ideally, all the decision-making groups in each part of a company will be involved at the earliest point when their views are relevant. Sometimes this amounts to more than thirty, but at least four or five in the smallest cases. Lining them up to act early throughout a process would minimise resistance later, to a buying decision, or to adoption or benefit delivery.

This is relevant to you if you serve businesses. Let's say the impact that you enable is urgent for them to achieve. Your offering becomes more strategic and demands increased involvement. Those clients need to remove decision-making bottlenecks preventing pace of adoption. Engaging them this way, you challenge clients in ways that improve strategic impact for them.

This is also relevant when selling to consumers. The impact of your offering could improve how they serve employers, family members, the community they sustain and the suppliers they buy from. Solve their critical needs and attach to a principle and source of urgency that they hold close to heart. If that's you, you're justified to educate customers about how to get more closely involved and decide sooner.

Use your team when planning for key customer or opportunity strategies.

Expose the best you have on offer and ask a diverse team for challenge to discover its limitations. This is a double-edged sword. As I've mentioned throughout this book, being inclusive is challenging and demands openness to critique. Outcomes are unpredictable. Such varied groups invariably have various opinions.

The effect could be to sharpen differentiation, or just expose weaknesses and threats. For you, this could mean muddying water where you previously imagined compelling opportunity. Acting upon what you discover, in the right way, is always an important choice. The scales tip easily in favour of this collaboration. The outcome could be to reinforce positives, to unearth negatives or maybe just to moderate an exaggerated positive to be more realistic. All these may be critical success factors.

A client workshop group discovered a winning strategy. They combined a little-known, low-price risk management software product with their mainstream data services. In that same workshop, they also identified a critical threat from a better and cheaper alternative from one of the client's adjacent market suppliers. I was shocked that their board of directors had known about this growing threat for several years and hadn't acted upon that knowledge.

The board opted to ignore the threat and asked salespeople to sell better. Whether they were naturally ostrich-like, or just choosing to defer the topic, the effect on the culture was long-lasting. This group felt unable or unwilling to restate that threat to their superiors. Future success could have relied on them doing so, yet a weakness in senior executives had pre-emptively scuppered any chances of that.

Consider what the world's been through: the uncertainty of a pandemic and job insecurity in a weakened economy. It would be even more difficult now to hope people will have the courage to speak up. It's the job of leadership to open themselves to that and give genuine attention to what is learned.

Never ignore an inconvenient truth. Take insights and feed them into your strategy forum. New knowledge feeds analysis models such as Five Forces, the Strategy Diamond and Five Horizons. Tough decisions are driven by strategic analysis. This client was an industry-leading company that failed, so any of us could fall victim to that misjudgement. Perhaps even someone you know.

> Choose frameworks and stick with them to expose gaps and differentiation. Establish a norm of method-based ways of working.

I've long known great benefit when sales teams work by a common methodology. More so when all people in all stages of go-to-market become fluent in the standard sales models and terminology.

Being professional in how you work with customers and orchestrate your go-to-market becomes a defendable differentiator that's difficult to copy. The customer confidence this inspires lasts longer than many other features. Having a common language, a norm of method-based ways of working in sales and delivery, and a standard model for challenging and supporting each other means the one pair of eyes handling a strategy can become twenty pairs of eyes.

The only obstacles to achieving this standardisation would be lack of trust, disrespect of humility or absence of common sense. You need to encourage others to accept that their success is just as worthy when they stand on the shoulders of colleagues. You need to demonstrate that, too.

Impact of models is multiplied by creating a cyclical feed combining company-level strategy with business readiness assessment and plans for product go-to-market, major market or client development, and opportunities. Lessons learned should be applied everywhere, from strategy to plans and, conversely, from plans to strategy, in a fluid way.

Avoid the shiny new method mentality
when new executives are hired.

Well-chosen executives arrive with fresh ideas that supplement what you've already done. Make sure they don't arbitrarily trash what's been created by predecessors. Experience shows it's not always methods and tools that are at fault.

Failure is more often from lack of reinforcement, lack of coaching and lack of hearing. Value generated in teams should be assimilated universally. Transfer of company-level insights helps those teams succeed. Fix that first.

There are features you should look for in such models. Rather than describing solutions for each, I'll focus on interactions between these topics and company-level go-to-market strategy.

The question is how you make this systemic for compliance and consistent use. Investors and acquirers long for this attribute, and it will be highly valued in any company pre-deal. That is one good way to sustainably increase company value. Make sure you know your ideal ways of working, then formulate models that you foresee will perpetuate success, and make them systematic and automated.

Take only the right CTMs – and ensure more of them succeed more quickly. Roughly 95% of new product CTMs fail, losing billions a year. By codifying models to mitigate causes of such failures, concept-to-market profits increase and companies are more highly valued. More immediately of interest is that you prevent frustration, wasted effort and losses from investing without getting the expected returns. There are numerous success factors for such a model, which highlight the positive effect it has on go-to-market success, and investor and acquirer attractiveness.

Listen better to your ecosystem landscape to discover ideas from employees, investors, commentators and analysts, suppliers and partners, customers and wherever else you might look. This reduces the chances of missing best ideas and settling on second best. If you're fishing in the right waters, you'll catch the best fish.

Invest in the most investable idea. Use a rational objective basis to choose. Avoid the trap of interpersonal preferences slipping in. You invest in fewer propositions delivering weak results. Set yourself a barrier to entry that rejects weaker ideas in the comfort zone and accepts potential game changers in unfamiliar spaces.

A framework should assess and help you improve attractiveness and ease to implement, strategic alignment, general marketplace and customer alignment, and alignment with positive or negative impact on the business.

If you fail to plan you plan to fail. Take a thorough go-to-market process model and scratch out the bits you believe aren't needed. Give the right tasks to all players from your ecosystem so your concept gets to market without nasty surprises. Co-create value opportunities based on known strategic priorities and impact. All these elements increase the chances of your new concepts being among the 5% succeeding, and not the 95% that fail.

Your proximity and familiarity with customers will improve everything that follows. Strong customer-centric culture is a clear predictor of success. This being systemic in your business complements company-level valuation.

In business-to-business this means building a norm to co-create value opportunities based on customer vulnerabilities or opportunities, their goals, initiatives and strategic direction. Align this well with capabilities you create for them better than competitors can. Interlock to make sure it improves your company-level strategy and individual sales deal strategies that spin off. In business-to-consumer, reconfirm the hypothesis of their needs, values and priorities.

Too many people bypass customers in product creation. It remains the same later in the lifecycle when supremely confident in a proposition. It's good to get back to walking the streets and finding that target segment, to test and validate or disprove assumptions, and that helps you to iterate the strategy.

Do that better. Demonstrate that all products and services focus on achieving a superb customer-experience journey. Prove consumers perceive greatest value. This translates into greater go-to-market performance. If such a practice is a virtuous habit in the company, positive valuation follows. Collaboratively create winning sales strategies to defeat competitors based on value.

Learn and apply lessons from why and how you win, and why you lose deals. This is one way of moving the abstract ideas of competitive strategy into the cold hard light of day. Make this part of your working rhythm. By doing so, you win more profitable and larger deals, and market share will accrue. Evidence of this way of working strengthens you in the eyes of investors.

These lessons need to be firmly impacted on company strategy in an intelligent way, quickly. Egos and defensiveness cannot feature in this process, so find a way to protect people when they admit things are not all perfect. Make sure company strategic choices are transferred into the sales deal strategy. Openness is a two-way street. Create action plans and ensure all people work consistently and compliantly. This is a basic precept of doing a good deal strategy better.

Make sure the people believe in the filter you create to decide which deals to walk away from. That is the best possible way to find those deals you should be working on. A company that spends more of its time working on winnable deals, and less on unwinnable ones, is a stronger business. Strategic clarity helps you achieve this.

In your internal rhythm, find a style of propositioning that encourages obsession with client business objectives. Make sure that your products and capabilities are not pushed unless value delivery is magnified. Doing this helps you cross-sell multiple products and services by adding to the business impact. It also prevents customer frustration were you to regurgitate product-speak.

If you struggle to get the attention of the senior people who you want to engage, you're not alone. Be honest, confront assumptions and plan to close gaps in your coverage of stakeholders. If you can't, then there's a good chance what you're offering or how you're offering it doesn't speak loudly enough in the language of the customer, and you won't succeed.

If you're successful in engaging and making an impact for senior stakeholders, that will become a business lever par excellence.

Unhelpfully brushing over people as being only 'the techy who just checks things over' or 'the president who just gives orders and the rubber stamp' is absolute nonsense. Strategy that works well helps you to ease open the door to those making buying decisions.

I've seen investment pitch decks that reveal a company's lax attitude towards competitors. It reveals a failing mode of thinking in which one predicts success is achieved by selling into customers harder. The habitual winners out there understand that their job is to beat the competitors, and that means all sources of competition. Choose a niche where you dominate competitors.

When a business embeds that practice and continually shares learning into company strategy and across sales teams, that company wins more often and is more highly valued.

Your strengths are only true strengths when an advantage of yours is simultaneously a competitor's weakness. It's only a differentiator when that is true against *all* sources of competition, and something customers all consider to be an important and compelling aspect of their need. Get that right in deals, apply it in the company strategy and across all competitive situations. Then you'll succeed.

Customers have antibodies to product- and vendor-lingo, and they far prefer people who talk *their* language. Learn and demonstrate customer-centred and impact-oriented messaging in value propositions. You will be embraced by customers, markets, investors alike. Staying product-bound and limited to echoing tag lines will cause you an uphill climb into the hearts and minds of customers.

Use all that you've learned about customers. Use words they use and not your jargon. Say less and make sure you drive home that what you offer is important for their high priority needs. Show that your differentiation, or strengths, are of compelling importance to their ability to succeed. Determine your whole business readiness to achieve sales success in go-to-market.

All these points are valuable in the cyclical exchange between individual plans and valuable company-level strategy.

Use insights to secure opportunities

Strategic sales leadership demands insight into all aspects of business readiness. Demonstrate a continuous improvement mindset, armed with a model for testing readiness. Constant re-evaluation, improvement planning and management of change will prove your readiness for maximum execution of strategy.

Assessment criteria generic to all businesses can be added to company specifics. That enables you to compare with industry benchmark metrics, and to know where you stand versus threshold and peer group comparison.

This should at least cover performance management, process uniformity and compliance, people enablers, system enablers, sales toolkit, developmental factors and routes-to-market. There are more, of course, which you can and should explore to decide how you will use and demonstrate use of continuous improvement. Subjective self-assessment is less highly valued than comparing against objective rationale-based criteria testing the most critical factors contributing to sales success.

A recurring theme here is to improve how you decide on the right action to take, and then make that happen. You've read about strategy models and the interlock between frameworks where these insights are massaged into company-level strategy. It's important that you keep the faith. It is not complicated, and it is valuable.

It's your choice whether to stay on the original track, course-correct or go off at a complete tangent. You could conclude it's better to fail fast and move on to something else. In the words of the Chinese Thirty-Six Stratagems, perhaps you will 'sacrifice the plum tree to preserve the peach tree'. In other words, a short-term goal could be sacrificed to achieve the longer-term win.[35]

Regardless of outcome, there is no value from taking a shortcut here. When analysis is thorough and candid, fuelled with insights gained from your team and their work, you will discover everything you need for success. The only missing piece is whether to 'just do it', or to shelve it and 'wait and see'.

Earlier, I told a story of a fictitious data and risk management company. In my story, the board had ignored insights into a new and disruptive threat from an adjacent sector. As is often the case, this wasn't confronted head-on as it should have been. When businesses fail to listen and fail to act upon insights, they end up defending in a market they may have previously led. Being inclusive and swift to act can enable them to leverage a successful differentiator, by forming a new integrated value proposition. Often, that is not done either.

Deflecting the puzzle for salespeople to reassemble, I've seen it take up to two years to react more formally. During that time only 10–20% of salespeople organically discover and use the differentiated sales approach. Such a company would sacrifice a large swathe of secure market share and sales opportunity.

---

35   en-academic, 'The Thirty-Six Stratagems'

Face truths you might otherwise ignore.

As mentioned previously, I occasionally guest lecture to the MBA cohort at WBS. The strategy professor and I agreed I'd use an entrepreneur case study to demonstrate how simple it is to gain value from analysis. We intentionally chose a case study from a market sector unfamiliar to all students.

This forced them to experience the power of not making snap judgements. In a person's own sector, often they short-circuit the strategy journey, imagining they know enough already. You may see that among colleagues when the time comes for strategic discussions. Keeping an open mind is difficult, but it's vital to balance old and new insights from varying reference points. Using an unfamiliar sector forces the cohort to immerse in models, and in doing so they experience their true power.

I've repeatedly used a case study based on a real client whom I advised to follow a course-corrected strategy, aiming to accelerate penetration and secure an ecosystem place of value. The founder, and more so his co-directors and shareholders, variously disagreed. Over a year passed before we spoke again. All MBA groups concluded the same advice. I had no idea what path the client had taken, but I was supremely confident of the advice.

In the intervening period, the founder was on the verge of securing the same go-to-market alignment that I, and the business school cohorts, had recommended.

In summary, this is the power of structured strategic analysis. Even those with no experience of a business sector have been consistently able to provide salient guidance that matched the conclusions of an experienced management team in real life. Part of the success of this comes from abandoning any desire to be the one who is right and asking others to challenge you and to allow themselves to be challenged.

Interlocking that structure across all forms of business processes enables strategic insight to be gained. That should be translated into company-level strategic analysis that a management team may then use to the business's advantage.

Create a predictable and consistent way of working and capture ideas that are created to cyclically influence strategic fine-tuning. If you find opportunities for change, you might press ahead in tell mode, or sacrifice efficiency to be inclusive and co-create. Only you will know how to do this and when to act, but the key result is to find the confidence that you're making the right decisions, and then get on with it.

10

Apply Better Energy, Better

Many people in leadership roles believe their ability to bring the energy out from a team is central to its success. In my experience, most of the times I hoped a clever idea was enough, it was only when the group gave all its energy that those ideas would come to fruition.

'The secret of change is to focus all your energy not on fighting the old but on building the new.'[36] You will gain the energy of your chosen group by doing the right things and building for a better future. Even if it feels like they misunderstand or resist at first, it is worth persisting to achieve collective commitment to your success.

The phrase 'bringing a strategy to life' implies that a spark, electricity, energy is needed. This is not something a leader does

---

36 This quote is often wrongly ascribed to Socrates, but it was in fact penned by Dan Millman and attributed to his childhood mentor, whom he nicknamed Socrates. It is nevertheless a good one-liner for my purposes: Quote Investigator, 'The Secret of change…'

to a team or to a market. You may have been told in secondary school science classes that energy is everywhere, mostly latent, waiting to be unlocked. Often, unlocking this among groups of people who tend not to spend their energy recklessly can be the make or break in any initiative.

Energy builds, or depletes, through levels of belief. This is true both for you and for those you wish to lead. It applies inside your business, across a market, or at the point in an ecosystem that offers potential for maximum gravitational pull that could help you mainstream.

There is real strength and differentiation to be gained from being attuned to how you might unlock and direct that energy and sense of belief. You can observe the effects of this and then influence the dynamics of groups to help you achieve your goals.

The power of self-belief

Early in my career, I was taught to notice the atmosphere when walking the corridors of a customer's offices. There, I might sense whether the mood was predictive of their success or demise. In doing so, I could qualify whether to work with them. Initially, I questioned both the logic and moral justification of this. Eventually, I learned this is something not to ignore. Their beliefs as individuals and their group dynamic predicted the outcome of their trajectory.

Think about any situation you can remember where a group faced impending peril. Consider whether a strong belief they would make it through improved their ability to grasp more options for success. Conversely, perhaps a sense of doom and likely failure might have caused a group to reach a self-fulfilling negative outcome.

I reflect on a time I transitioned from 'individual contributor' to manager, and later became a mentor of other managers. I discovered that success is only in part determined by the power of differentiation and effectiveness of delivery. Victory depends on the confidence and belief of each person, and how likely they are to make maximum effect as a cohort. It is determined by the choices people make together and the energy they apply on a minute-by-minute basis.

In other words, the energy they apply almost entirely dictates the impact they make with the tools you provide them. It stands to reason that you need to fine-tune and improve your effectiveness in this critical aspect of leadership. Even if you've been led to believe this is a matter of charisma, it's not true. There are forces at play in group dynamics, and you can learn how to guide these to your advantage.

The power of belief is a great force for success, even in hopeless situations. A memorable moment of success resulting from belief can be a self-perpetuating legend.

Except for a few younger years in California, I grew up in Bootle, Liverpool. At the age of seventeen, I moved to Johannesburg. For anyone who knows what Liverpool is famous for, it won't surprise you that I know the words to a few Beatles, McCartney and Lennon songs.

In Liverpool, it is practically a duty to follow either Liverpool or Everton in the national sport. I feel obligated to use Liverpool Football Club as a case study – so here it is. Even those who are not followers of this sport will still find the valuable point made through this example.

Liverpool faced Milan at the 2005 UEFA finals in Istanbul. At half-time, Liverpool had scored zero to Milan's three goals. The team descended to face their coaches in a dire state. My father remained in self-imposed exile in a bedroom. He feared that real-time match updates could kill him through stress. A friend from South Africa, attending the match as a corporate guest, decided to leave the stadium at that point. Everyone believed the disappointment of Liverpool to be inevitable.

The half-time break was time well spent. Within ten minutes, the Liverpool captain had scored dramatically. One could sense something had changed in the team. Supporters were somehow coming back to life. It was hope, belief. There was an inkling that they only needed to give themselves permission to feel confident.

Two minutes later, this was followed by another Liverpool goal. Then, after another four minutes, a third Liverpool goal. What I watched was spine-tingling. A life lesson par excellence. Belief? There it was.

Two of the world's most formidable teams, equalling the highest standards of fairness and professionalism, in a competition based on skill and self-belief. In that second half, and in the extra thirty minutes, and in the subsequent penalty shoot-out, it was self-belief that differentiated the winners.

Many would argue that skill allows one team to beat all others and make their success unstoppable. Consider whether that has always been the case in your competitive environment; it's seldom been true in my world. I've seen too many disappointed teams, whose customers chose competitors despite them having superior offerings and capabilities.

It could be fair to assume that capability superiority results in victory, but facts dispute that. Liverpool's arch-rivals, Manchester United, having been nearly unbeatable, endured humiliation after changing management. Liverpool has a reputation for disproving this idea. It's generally accepted that, even during years when theirs was a less competent team, through spirit and belief in each other they succeeded. Conversely, they have been caught off guard in times of disillusionment, defeated by far less capable teams. I use this sporting parallel because it is resoundingly applicable to business.

Even when facing life-and-death situations,
self-belief can make all the difference.

As a young man, I sailed a poorly equipped twenty-seven-foot Westerly Merlin yacht. I was accompanied by my then girlfriend, her mother and her father, the amateur captain. Setting off from Lavrion, in Greece, our poorly qualified 'captain' never revealed even the slightest doubt in his ability to succeed. On the return leg of our trip, the Aegean turned nasty. With the winds too powerful for our sailing skills, we took a defensive decision to surf the waves and rely on our strong inboard diesel engine.

My dear friend and captain calmly took me aside to show me the fuel indicator. It was perilously close to empty. Silently tapping his nose, he suggested we keep this to ourselves, whispering, 'Fear is the fastest way to fail, so let's keep this quiet and handle it ourselves... there's nothing to be gained by worrying them too soon.'

I look back at this, and realise his recklessness was outrageous. Especially in the face of danger, he was of course wrong to decide on behalf of two women what they were entitled to know.

I do distinctly remember, however, that for the remainder of the trip I felt strangely confident. None of us deviated from focusing on where we'd 'inevitably' find our solution. That continued until seeing the lights of a safe mooring and tying up for a good night's sleep.

Earlier in my career, I was privileged to take leadership roles that included transformational technology programmes with national health services. Among my team were people who had worked with health clients for longer terms than their counterparts there who provided healthcare to patients. Their dedication was firmer than I've seen in all other sectors and companies. Often personal tragedies or experiences caused these people to have passionate belief in the need for better healthcare, and a commitment to fulfilling that need. I knew this team would never walk away from a challenge.

Due to impossible client conditions, the firm had thus far failed to deliver the desired results. Numerous vendors and systems integrators began to falter. After six years running multibillion IT programmes, I personally know many key personnel from those other companies, who were new to health ICT and passing through seeking profit and career kudos. Their resolve was not as firm as ours.

One by one, several global companies withdrew shamefaced, resigning from their obligations to the client. Severe shareholder value impact and the 'impossibility' of the challenge was their justification. In private, they admitted that key personnel could not sustain the negative pressure of persistent failures. I saw the opposite, from the board of directors and shareholders down to each team member. Not once did I hear a believable suggestion that we could walk away from that commitment to national healthcare transformation.

To understand the impact of that, let's put this into perspective of what was at risk and what was to be gained. In a population of 66 million, roughly 25 million work in private and nonprofit sectors, with 5 million working in the public sector. Public sector revenues in the UK are over $400 billion at time of writing. Depending on who you ask, around 10% of the addressable ICT market then was in the public sector. That is a huge market with a lot to gain by being trusted.

Their belief and passion to deliver resulted in short-term shareholder losses, which you might argue was harmful. In hindsight, positive change was achieved, and lives were saved. That is a market where people have long memories and tend to reward those who help them succeed. Many there were safeguarded by that company's commitment. They know which partner won't turn and run the next time.

We live in a world where many feel unable to speak up, and less able to demand good corporate moral fibre. Boards refuse to listen to and learn from the wisdom of their people. In this case, it was spirit, belief and determination that won the day.

The impact of losing self-belief

Call it positive energy, negative energy or atmosphere. It doesn't matter how many sweet rewards someone is offered, they won't run into the unknown darkness to climb a hill unless they want to. If they start begrudgingly, then if they ever do reach the top, many others who were more motivated will be there first.

In the aftermath of catastrophes, there has always been a costly low in energy. Living for so many years in South Africa, I observed the effect on normal people of having lived close to random acts of violence. The result was emotional numbing, demotivation and a focus on the short-term rather than long-term potential. Despite the illusion of an energetic and enthusiastic culture, often this was helping to conceal feelings of deflated energy.

Since then, in catastrophes or events that take the whole world unprepared, I've observed something similar. As though we all think as one, there can be a sapping of energy as a chain reaction slows down the world. It happened after the 2004 train bombings in Madrid and the Indian Ocean earthquake and tsunami just after Christmas in the same year; after the 2005 terror bombings in London and the 9/11 attacks on the Twin Towers; and it followed the shock effects of global financial collapse in 2008 and the surprise results in the UK's Brexit vote.

It is as if we are on a finely balanced knife-edge, even if optimism is high and life going to plan. It seems our main protection is to keep energy high and positive. These days, I know to anticipate that such issues will inevitably arise occasionally. Even though world events can't be predicted, one can study people and be prepared to influence them to avoid the lows. Disasters and less severe disappointments will always arrive. That's life. How you respond is down to personal choice. As a leader, you affect the way others feel through your actions and influence. They will directly change the outcome for your business and the impact on the lives of those depending on it.

Watch out for the perils of divided leadership.

For our entire history, the military has faced this challenge. Variously, the threat comes from the presence of emperors or empresses, kings or queens, dictators of other origins, elected leaders or career civil servants. You might not know this, but military leaders prefer to reduce conflict and focus on avoiding death or injury. They have always been the shield protecting personnel from the trigger-happy whims and counter-strategic dictates of those who have no experience in the theatre of conflict.

A bond of trust is vital, and achieved when people know leaders' instructions are safe, well-reasoned and necessary. If they believe that to be the case, personnel will do as they're told. A fine balance is required to ensure success and respect the superiority of elected officials, or multiple sources of authority.

Expert leaders translate unpredictable policies into realistic success strategies that their people will believe in and follow to the end.

This is a useful reminder that the belief of your people, customers, market and ecosystem, once achieved, is not guaranteed indefinitely. You will seldom lead in isolation and there will always be influences threatening to dilute yours. A company's leadership must stay vigilant and present a cohesive, unified persona that reinforces this level of belief, positive energy and trust.

Beware the energy depleter

Cultures evolve and motivation levels become a feature of that. Team culture is an evolving human and social dynamic. Motivation levels can be a consequence of a cultural response to changing circumstances. As this stems from within, it cannot easily be wilfully changed from above or outside, which leads us to the question of whether and how you can influence team motivation or even change their culture.

Consider taking a long walk with children. They will seldom follow a straight line directly to where you want them to go. With occasional nudging, accepting that they will go this way then that, you're more likely to get to where you planned to be. The same is true of the dynamics of groups that you hope to influence. Forcing a straight line of change is likely to result in frustrated failure. The complexities of how to influence a team or, worse still, a market to follow your desired direction can feel insurmountable.

It is obvious why, considering these are collectives of individuals, each with their own egocentric view. You are only one person, in a group of perhaps thirty, fifty or a hundred others. Add their families, friends and external influences on top of that, and soon you see that your ability to force a direct impact has a lot of competition.

Energy builders and energy depleters make
more impact than you can alone.

There are many techniques you can use in this field; for example, team-building rah-rah events or shared learning tackling tough issues. Here are a few fresh ideas that strike me as being powerful, not only at work but elsewhere in life too.

I ran a survey online to test attitudes towards using team building as an opportunity to focus on projects which supported a worthy cause or charity. Over 90% supported this idea, stating clearly that they would prefer to help a worthy cause than endure another meaningless rah-rah event. I have certainly experienced huge motivational gains by identifying a powerful sense of shared purpose for teams.

My survey discussion thread was hijacked by an 'energy depleter' in our midst. He insisted that the only way for team building to succeed was through traditional, physically or mentally demanding activities taking people out of their comfort zones. Sadly, he missed the point, which was that both aims can be achieved. The added benefit of being purpose-led is to strengthen a common sense of meaning in the team. The same is achieved by attaching purpose to the brand in a business's go-to-market efforts.

It's critical not to fall victim to the unchecked negative effect of depleters. Spend time observing the influencers in your environment. Who gets the most 'influencing airtime'? What is their nature? Are they a builder of the positive or a depleter? Whose influence do you choose to amplify and reinforce? Can you affect how other people interpret and process these various influencers?

Give more airtime to the positive –
the Disney positivity propaganda bonanza.

In the US, there is a positivity propaganda engine second to none. The impression this creates reinforces a national culture that is now perceived globally to thrive on aspiration, positivity and vibrant personalities.

It is almost of secondary importance whether that truly reflects the living reality of all Americans. The effect on the public and on the brand 'US' is one of viral motivation.

I recall an international seminar where the facilitator asked each delegate to introduce themselves and how they were feeling about being there. When it came to the turn of a twenty-three-year-old American, she said enthusiastically, 'My name is Alice, and I'm on fire, I think this is absolutely awesome, and I'm stoked.' He went on to the next delegate, from the Netherlands, who, after removing his flabbergasted expression, said, 'Err… well, I'm Peter. How am I feeling? Not bad, but to be honest I'm not sure why I'm here or what I will gain from it.'

I'm not suggesting one is more motivated than the other; I don't know. Nor is it clear who learned more from the seminar. What is clear, though, is that the former, in all her brashness, may build positives before negatives, or at least that seemed to be the case. The latter, Peter, more likely will urge people to think carefully before talking positively and could deplete or emphasise the negatives. This is useful to know. Listening to how people speak among teams often reveals these traits.

One should at least be aware of who is dominating the airtime in your environment. Understand their types, styles and motives. A cautious doubter – maybe like my smart Alec from Chapter 8 – may become a powerful advocate. Equally, a vocal cheerleader could conceal negativity expressed privately and could secretly be a snake in the grass. Beware.

> Always build up. Never deplete. The world
> will take care of the depleting for you.

Malcolm Gladwell, in his book *Blink*, claimed one can observe whether couples will or won't succeed within a few seconds of watching them interact. Expand this to relationships of all kinds, at work, too. You will see that Malcolm's theory has legs.[37]

He wrote that if one partner depletes the other partner's confidence or self-worth, bringing them down a notch, that is a sign of trouble to come. If one partner builds up the other partner, boosting and promoting qualities, that is a good thing. The latter 'builder' traits should be instinctive in a life partner. If 'depleter' traits show up, then that person is showing either thinly veiled disdain, or deep-seated insecurity.

The same is true in attitudes people show towards fellow employees, extended family, sports teams, work groups and companies. All these groups offer incentives to support and reinforce, yet so often there is criticism and depletion. The effect can become an infectious destructive process. Conversely, if turned to focus on the positive, the effect can become a success booster.

The world has a way of knocking us down, to teach hard lessons. We don't need a manager, colleague, relative or life partner doing that too. The different impacts of these human builder or depleter personas are precursors to the motivation or demotivation of a unit, and thereby to its success or failure.

---

37   Gladwell, *Blink*

Observe your team closely and form a handling strategy. People need to hear the builders more than they hear the depleters. Make sure you amplify them. Decide to focus people on the outcomes from reinforcing the positive.

Your aim is to create a network of evangelists as described in Chapter 8. When this happens, people will reach a state of mind where they search out and echo the builders. Teach keen influencers techniques to do this, and coach your managers to be coaches. They will understand that allowing depleters to influence them leads to a negative performance and has a negative interpersonal effect. Teach them, instead, to spot depleters and influence them towards emphasising the positive. This creates motivational antibodies.

Coaches will spend time with people discussing helpful and productive outlooks, and they are skilled in confronting the opposite positively. If they encounter disagreement, a coach may uncover attitudes or issues preventing consensus. They know it's a valuable lesson to listen genuinely and keep an open mind to changing their point of view. This helps them discover what they need to do when eventually deciding on a better way. Showing commitment to people at a personal level, without judgement, will build trust and help them succeed.

The good news is that once people experience this, they replicate it. That helps them to reinforce positive builders through coaching depleters positively, and it becomes a self-fulfilling prophecy of success.

In summary, in any productively motivated environment, the builders tend to have more cultural influence than the depleters do. Leaders become coaches. People discover the many virtues and personal value of being builders in all parts of their lives. Success becomes habitual, even addictive, as these positive legends emerge as the most prevalent influence. The great thing is that this all begins with you.

Groups of people in teams or across ecosystems begin to handle difficulties before they arise, overcoming complexity in projects and tackling their business objectives differently. This is because they form a deeply held belief that they can succeed better as builders.

That is the 'energy factor'. Many old-style leaders prefer to value 'charismatic energy transfer' for leadership. This fails to leverage the most potent and sustainable source of personal and team energy, which comes from within people, emerging as belief in the common purpose, and self-motivation.

11

Principles-Led Is
A Differentiation

People, and by ripple effect whole markets too, will buy into your purpose, values and beliefs. You need to define and amplify these ideals.

Perhaps you've wondered why most assume that a doctor is trustworthy and will probably provide the best possible solution when help is needed for health issues. Even if you've never read it, you might know about the Hippocratic oath that every doctor must take. If the doctor fails to maintain that commitment, they will be struck off the list that permits them to practise their profession.

That element of trust is a differentiator for the profession. Arguably even for those who don't know of the oath's existence, that brand value of trustworthiness has slipped into assumptions globally. I'd strongly recommend you read the modern version of that oath. Imagine your company being attached to such a principle, to never knowingly do harm, and to seek out the most expeditious path to do good.[38]

You will gain rewards, internally, with colleagues and in the market. Even children will understand you better when your purpose and values magnify the true impact of what you do and how well you do it.

Decide your beliefs, the meaning and purpose for everything you do. If you doubt there's a valid purpose, you might suddenly notice it's under your nose.

In the eyes of buyers and employees, your beliefs are as important as what you do and how you do it. If you imagine it's good enough to just have a great product, think again. It's never been enough. There has always been a little extra something that causes people to give their loyalty. Don't be mistaken: unless you want to sell to a newcomer every day of your life, loyalty is vital.

I worked with a reputable and successful producer of international adverts and movies in an Eastern European country. He wanted to understand how this concept could possibly differentiate his business. He went through cycles of ideation and competing for project funding in a blow-by-blow battle versus other equally qualified production companies. While doing so, he churned through staff, with a maximum retention of two years.

---

38   Marks, 'Medical definition of Hippocratic oath'

His initial resistance faded into enlightened acceptance. He did indeed have principles and values that differentiated, and perhaps these would cause others to gravitate to him. In private, he'd already expressed a desire that he hoped for greater harmony between ethnicities in his country. He wanted to improve local capabilities through collaboration and open sharing of skills between ethnicities and language groups. He also reflected on how his company uniquely supported gender equality, promoting women into technical and creative roles better than competitors had.

As I've noted repeatedly, principles- and purpose-led strategy, resilience and sustainability don't just mean environmentalism or climate. For my intention here, they mean anything that we choose to stand up for, which might be valued by others. If sufficiently differentiated and well reinforced, this might take effect and create loyalty that could result in market segment leadership.

In our past, the advertising industry promised us they can successfully 'teach' customers what to value. Consequently, people rightly felt brainwashed into believing they valued features. In the case of the movie producer, this led to him repeating a stereotypical competitive approach. Yet, by reinforcing the importance of capabilities and service excellence features that are inevitably present in most or all competitors, he wasn't succeeding.

That kind of feature battle was never satisfying. Neither customer nor suppliers felt they received the value they desired. In future, the tables will be turned. Smart marketers will reflect the principles and values that are held most dear in the hearts of customers and employees. That will connect with loyalty in markets. Features will be tested as a matter of course, but one's values create competitive advantage. This awakening is long overdue.

What do human beings really want?

Perhaps you can't yet explain the principles your business will reinforce, or the ideals, causes or social movement you align with. You'd better figure that out, and soon.

If you doubt this, do a bit of digging for results of recent consumer polls. You'll see, as I did, a myriad of issues that people care about deeply. Customers are telling you that within ten years resilience and sustainability will be the only option for business to create competitive advantage. That is what people care about most of all. Absence of a response to those questions will be viewed as ignorance.

We no longer pray at the altar of growth for its own sake. We now seek resilience and sustainability. To be allowed into the competition for business you will first need to prove you're able to do what you do without damaging the ability of future generations to sustain their needs. Maybe you can make a net improvement, which is a bonus, as therein you can find many opportunities for a purpose that markets will value.

There is evidence that traditional mainstream businesses are awakening to this reality. Earlier, I mentioned UppyBags – a brand that has adhered to as many positive virtues of sustainability as possible. At the time of writing, I've been made aware that one of the largest department store chains in Spain has contacted the brand owner to enquire about partnering to retail these bags as part of a project to promote their brand's alignment with sustainability values.

This is a solid example of where ethical brand values are becoming critical for consumer marketing executives. The department store chain cleverly decided to leverage the accumulated brand equity of UppyBags and of other sustainable product brands.

I once saw a rather embarrassing moment splashed across the press, where a well-known brand of mayonnaise was unfairly mocked for grandstanding a poorly conceived brand purpose. Admittedly, theirs was a clumsy attempt to jump aboard the trend train. They didn't properly consider what form of purpose would matter and would be taken seriously by their consumers. Markets and media concluded that their purpose message was more likely intended to distract consumers from the firm's profit focus, which they failed to achieve.

I asked a friend recently whether a brand's sustainable message would cause her to switch. She said no, not necessarily. I rephrased my question to ask, 'What if a new brand came along and educated you about the harm done to communities in Vietnam by the shoe industry, and then presented a brand that makes its purpose to do good there instead?' This ordinary consumer paused to think for a moment, turned and said, 'Oh yes, I get it, I think I know what you're getting at now – yes, I probably would change brands.' I rest my case.

Here's a task for you – a little homework. Ask a few people who work for you from the Millennials and Gen Z why you are the company they chose to work for. Then ask them what might cause them to work for someone else. Besides a good test of trust and openness, this should reveal something to you about their values and the basis of future employment choices. Keep asking why, digging deeper. You will discover either the values connecting them to you or the values they are looking for elsewhere.

Another task. Ask five customers of the same generation similar questions, but this time about their buying choices. Don't accept a feature or pricing as a valid reply. After their first answers, dig deeper and keep on asking. Show true curiosity to get to the root of it with them. In doing so, you will find the purpose, meaning or principle that underpins their choices. It could be that you discover the reasons why they could change once a viable alternative is available from a company that better reflects their values.

Allow yourself to be amazed. Of course, it could be that you discover your target employees and customers are far shallower than you'd thought – more price- or feature-oriented than their generational peer group – but I think not. Sooner or later in such conversations, all people reveal why they chose to do what they do for a living, or how they decide where to buy what they consume.

The bitter reality is that ignoring the issue won't help. They will discover that they're not getting what they really want, while you have mismatched values. That creates a sense of emptiness that craves satisfaction. Once an option exists that satisfies that craving, it will drive their future choices, material purchases, employment and consumption. Once that happens, it rarely changes.

This is important. Whether you're large or small, there are transferable lessons to be learned from the experience of others.

A meaning and purpose are easier to understand, and likely to cause loyalty. Important principles create closeness or distance with employees and customers.

I have done work in the past to develop integration benefits for companies when acquiring others. This once involved a global brand and a large US-based competitor they were acquiring in a highly sensitive regulatory situation to avoid anticompetitive outcomes. These projects are interesting as they demonstrate the importance of values and principles being matched to achieve synergies and gains.

Typically, all bets are off as they seek innovative ways to make some gains from the high price tag they're about to pay. That should be easy. In one case, we knew there were innovations that were sure to offer global transformational impact. What we observed was quite the opposite. Cultures and values clashed, and this slowed acceptance of ideas across the division between the two.

The acquiring company was renowned for trust. Consumers had learned they could expect the best corporate values and that the board would diligently fulfil obligations to stakeholders and the environment. Employees universally valued those principles as a key motivator for choosing to work there.

The brand of the acquired company was globally renowned for a different reason. Their acquisition brought with it several lawsuits for malfeasance, including practices harmful to many thousands of customers. Although executives had the desire to make a positive impact, it seemed that, in practice, profit did come first and last, true to the twentieth-century paradigm. It seemed externally to consumers, internally to new colleagues and to shareholders that the only genuine strategic motivation there was profit-centric.

Whereas we identified huge benefit potential, this was counteracted by risk of legal costs and negative brand impact. From Germany to India and Japan, to the US and Latin America, reverberations shook the acquiring company's confidence. Continuity of the deal became the topic of debate at more than one board meeting.

Doors opened after deal closure which permitted open sharing of information. We observed executives from the acquired company being side-stepped. Those in the European acquirer sometimes swept aside their ideas and we could see no rational reason for this. World-beating innovations and capabilities were ignored, and, controversially, that was by a team that had previously freely embraced the value of integrating acquired companies.

It was apparent this reaction came from people rejecting other people. Considering many possible causes, I concluded this was due to negative perceptions and cultural antibodies arising from conflicting values. This was the fall-out from acquiring a brand that lacked values that the acquirer's executives held closest to their hearts.

From my third-party experienced viewpoint, I could see that these people were defending something more precious than egos – they were defending principles.

Being purpose-led makes a difference
in all sorts of ways.

If you look at publicly available research, this will be easy for you to verify. Putting in the effort to become a purpose-led business pays dividends. I'll quote specifics that have been tested and published widely.

Something that I can relate to is success in transformation efforts. Purpose-oriented companies experience 52% success in major transformation programmes, compared with 16% in those not led by specific purpose. The same is true of successful product launches: an astounding 56% compared with 33%. Of purpose-oriented companies 52% experienced greater than 10% growth, compared with 42% of companies not driven by purpose. Purpose-led companies achieved 66% global expansion, versus 48% for those not purpose-led.[39]

If existing employees and markets don't see eye to eye with you about your principles, they won't follow your ideas for new ways of working or new products. No matter how you carve up the numbers, the numbers stack up to prove this point.

You're creating a legacy of what future generations will say about your impact. You may have heard the idea of testing a pitch or elevator message on your grandparents, or on a child. If you can gain acceptance or excitement, you've done a good job. It's worth keeping that in mind when considering all strategic choices.

At a young age, my son announced to his teachers that his daddy was a secret police officer. I promise he'd invented it as a fantasy. I really was not a secret police officer. He had revealed that my work lacked meaning in his innocent mind. My work was, and probably still is, a mystery to my children.

---

39   Brower, 'The power of purpose and why it matters now'

My son's formative mind revealed something we all increasingly desire. He hoped that my job had some meaning and purpose. I'm sorry to say much of my life has been given over to matters of less consequence than if I were safeguarding our society. On occasion, I have risen to achievements of public worth, but I dare say my children would struggle to associate me with those. Only a few people would conclude I'd made a particular difference in the world.

Maybe that doesn't bother you too much now but, eventually, you might take that more seriously, as I do. This idea connects us all. If we are to be remembered, and there's no guarantee we will be after the dust settles, we all care about how and why this will be. Leaving behind us something of meaning as a legacy might be more important than you had thought up to now.

It's possible you don't care how your life's work is perceived, or about the consequences of your actions. If not, then your chances look poor, as customers and employees start to put your principles and purpose-led outlook to the acid test.

Your impact is important and matters
more than what you do, and how.

Some of the most meaningful performances of my life have not exactly looked as elegant as a ballet; instead, I'd say they resembled scrapping it out in fields of mud, dragging animals to shelter. You may have lived a life obsessing about looking as awesome at what you do as you possibly can. If so, this new competitive dynamic might feel as though it's exaggerating the importance of purpose.

Maybe telling yourself, 'I do this very, very well' has made a good marketing impact before, but that won't remain the same for much longer.

I am reminded of how chaotic it could have appeared when our team led the turnaround of a new outsourced network service provider for government. We all knew that no photos captured our sacrifice, and biographers would never write about our courage and commitment. Thank goodness – it would not have been a pretty sight, but that didn't matter. All that mattered to anyone in our team and the customer was the reason why it was important.

The infrastructure we created was a stepping stone that bolstered confidence and encouraged wider investment. Subsequently, others were able to create software and services that would save the lives of thousands: systems that prevented patients from toxic poisoning after being overprescribed conflicting medications by different clinicians, that secured online sharing of X-ray and MRI images nationwide, and other similar breakthrough capabilities.

This, we knew, was the reason why. It more than adequately justified all the terrible ninety-hour weeks, and the ugliness and clumsiness of working out how we completed the tasks. As a result, we did the right things, and we did them for the right reasons. Others knew this and each person involved knew it too. The value of that recognition will last longer than the lack of elegance in functional delivery might have appeared then.

Invite an imaginary child into the boardroom
while you make strategic choices.

Consider something the next time you are discussing strategic choices: you could, and hopefully soon will, be debating a company-level change to make an impact for the better, or to avoid impacting things for the worse. Remember the effect of the Hippocratic oath on the brand equity of clinicians and the effect on any individual that contravenes that obligation. How simple it is to step forward in that manner, yet how special it is to find firms that embody commitment to never knowingly do harm and always aim to do good.

It could mean shaving a fraction from bottom-line profits to achieve your values-based strategy. That will be your first step to gaining increased profit by moving from a growth-only precept towards a focus on societal resilience-first that will produce improved profits. You'll need belief, not only in the chances of gained profit, but also the certainty that absence of this could be disastrous for you.

Imagine, for a moment, that you've invited a child to the boardroom and given them an equal voice. Children look at things through an unfiltered lens. Their future is their now. They judge things on a different basis. Your excuses to delay won't convince them. By doing this, you personify imaginary future employees and future customers sitting in the room with you. Listen.

Think what a child would tell you, about whether your plans make sense. Imagine you're being studied from the moral superiority and future-clarity of a child. Then decide whatever you were about to decide. Do so in full knowledge that the child will hold you accountable. Before 2030 that accountability will decide your level of success, and your survivability during the Great Shift.

The ripple effect is real, and your choices
will affect others widely.

Accept it's possible, while not guaranteed, that what you do could be changing the world. You should first understand how ideas travel once they're shared, be that for good or bad. The simplest ideas in conversation then become resources for other creative minds to express ideas that amplify your own. In the minutes, days, months and years ahead, their creativity and inherent urge to communicate provides an accelerator effect. If you're purposeful, imagine what effects this could have for you.

Institutionally, companies and markets carry ripples and this stems from ideas created by individuals. Methodology I created has since become standard practice and terminology in companies that didn't even pay me for it. Employees there later imagined their company invented it. Of course, plagiarism is a great compliment. Theirs was unintentional and I didn't confront it. Even if I did take exception, I lacked horsepower to fund confrontation. It does demonstrate, however, how quickly and uncontrollably strong ideas can spread and take root once shared.

Six degrees of separation

I never imagined I would be able to influence the office of the president of the US. I experienced this from one employment decision when the team I joined decided to contact the global second in command for sponsorship of my large project, and I discovered an unintentional proximity to a member of the presidential strategic advisory team. I sat there, four levels removed from the president, and my ideas were being promoted and debated in that interconnected circle.

The theory of six degrees of separation states that we are, at most, six relationship connections away from any other person in the world. In fact, a study at Massachusetts Institute of Technology in 1961 concluded that in a US-sized population any two people can connect via at most two intermediaries. With a population of billions that might strike you as a bold presumption, but it's been tested and repeatedly proven to be true.[40]

It doesn't require a huge leap of the imagination to see that an idea received by my colleague, and enthusiastically promoted to the sponsor, is then shared over dinner with his colleague, the chair. Nor is it hard to imagine this idea might one day find its way to the ear of the president, in conversation with foreign dignitaries. This is the power of affinity. That is how realistic it could be that your actions and words can influence anyone in the world; eventually, potentially, everyone. Never underestimate the power of gossip, more so in times of uncertainty, and how this is then reinforced by myth-busting.

Urban myths spread more vigorously than boring old truths. Whether information is factual or sensationally false, it seems to have little bearing on how far it travels. Indeed, the phenomenal speed at which falsehoods spread through the rumour mill proves that less truthful but more shocking rumours are more likely to spread. This adds weight to the urgency that you should get started. Once you have decided upon the virtuous messaging you wish to promote, start spreading the word.

---

40   Travers and Milgram, 'An experimental study of the small world problem'

Worse still is that during times of uncertainty false rumours are more likely to be received as being equivalent of facts. We don't know if this is due to anxiety, or a need for certainties, but when a lot of emotion is at play the need for evidence tends to reduce. When humanity is understood this way, you see the risk of failing to put a truthful message out there staking claim to a principle or purpose-driven brand value. Anyone who acts first may be believed, perhaps regardless of their truthfulness.

Modern expansion on rumour and gossip theories has exposed a problem with myth-busting, where you later try to deny and incontrovertibly disprove a false rumour. That will result in cementing the falsehood as a truth in the minds of people. Familiarity breeds belief, or in other words, repetition causes people to believe. The prevalence of greenwashing that was described in Chapter 5 adds even greater urgency.[41]

Those acting with righteous intentions, building resilience and sustainability into supply chain ecosystems, should act soon to capture brand equity.

Ideas you put out there might well reach *all* people in the world through multiple paths of interconnectedness we all share. Competitors can achieve the same, spreading falsehoods, or perhaps truths, that defeat you by beating you to the market. That is thought-provoking.

---

41   Rosnow and Foster, 'Rumor and gossip research'

Find the social effect in your sector,
where it originates, how far it reaches.

One can't deny the importance of emotions that drive human choices. Ideas tugging at emotional triggers can cause a change in attitude and decision-making. This can travel far more rapidly than heaps of dry facts. Those spreading falsehoods do this; those with righteousness should do, too.

When it comes to understanding how segments of the target market respond to any form of influence, an obstacle is that sectors are just randomly assembled people. Each person is apparently unique, or so we are led to believe. When considering shared values and principles, the viewpoint changes.

By using persona-based segmentation, target market segments contain people with shared experiences, goals or motivations. Arguably, this is an opportunity to fine-tune better than merely using demographics. Tapping into shared principles or values of a segment helps find ways to create long-lasting connection there.

Consider how a segment responded previously to emotion-based stimulus. That could be a theme emerging rapidly, a major crisis or socioeconomic event. This allows you to compare them with other segments, to learn in hindsight and study the chain of influence, cause and effect. Check which personas said what. Ask if they were positive or negative. Follow how that cascaded to affect the segment. You could similarly do this to investigate a major client and their cultural reaction to proposed transformation, restructuring or new concept launches.

I referred to builder and depleter personas in Chapter 10. You will see there are influencers that have these effects in a segment or a company. You will observe the propensity of groups to respond to a positive or negative stimulus more forcefully. You will find pathways of social influence effects. By observing how the ecosystem has responded in the past, you are equipping yourself to predict the future.

For decades, respected scientists and activists have spoken with clarity. Using factual evidence, they informed us about the climate change we're experiencing, yet voices of misinformation and denial seemed sufficient to soothe the world into continuing unchanged. Consider the weight of that evidence. Then observe the inertia among a vast majority in the mainstream. This showed us that there can be overall low reactivity to these change drivers, and is a good example to consider.

Among the industrial power base, climate deniers may have been viewed as builder personas, enabling industry to continue uninterrupted. For environmentalists, these same forces would have been seen as depleters, obstacles in the path of solving a crisis.

Since 2018 we've seen mixed reactions to emotive outbursts from teenager Greta Thunberg. Perhaps unfairly, many in older generations reacted with sarcasm towards Greta, who was portrayed as a pushy youngster. Unfair because, after all, at worst she is a caricature of all teenagers who will be adults in a few years.[42]

---

42 Democracy Now, 'School strike for climate'; University of British Columbia, '2021 honorary degree recipients: Greta Thunberg'

The ideas behind urgency in environmentalism were not created by Greta, just delivered by her rather effectively. In doing so, she has performed the vital role of an emotion trigger, the effect of which we can study in different segments.

Don't attach to the idea of Greta, as that could cause bias from her being liked or disliked as an individual. Step back and consider the reaction to all eco-activists, those who blocked roads or confronted the establishment. You will observe a wave of protest that amounts to a social movement. This allows you to distinguish between segments, perhaps even people by name, based on their responses to such principles-based messages.

How did the mainstream react? With a little inconvenience to their commute, there were many who behaved as though they shared a vested interest in the politics of denial. Vocally, people rejected the movement as a depleter force that threatens the economy.

In other segments you see how this movement accelerated and how that translated into changing demand patterns. Look closely and you'll observe links and chains of influence as they cascade.

Such change patterns, and early sharing of ideas, will gather momentum and mass, eventually reaching a tipping point that is predictive of the Great Shift. Analysis could reveal who is most sensitive to principles-oriented messages, the segment whose buying and employment choices will be affected first, and the segment which will show delayed acceptance of emerging shifts in ways of thinking. It is only a question of when, not if, the majority will follow these earliest segments who make that shift.

That was an easy example. With more sophisticated enquiry you will hopefully find a link with sensitivity to similar dramatic influences, and how to improve your ability to access markets.

With open curiosity and willingness to listen, you may discover their opinions and gain influence enabling you to affect future demand patterns and employment choices.

A few years from now, these won't be 'the younger generations' anymore; they will be 'the majority of our customers and employees'. You need to stop asking whether it's worthwhile and start asking how you plan to survive if you don't do this.

In summary, defining a purpose and the principles underpinning your business creates attraction and loyalty among customers and employees far greater than simply proving you do a good job. By capturing an identity connected to this and leveraging the propensity of humans to spread words virally, you can and should aim to reach further and faster with that brand impact.

The legacy you leave behind you should matter now, and showing that you care about that will have surprisingly positive effects in the market today. Showing disregard will have the opposite effect, the impact of which might only become truly visible once a competitor steps forward decisively while you fail to do so.

You can find those elements in your business ecosystem that will amplify positive and negative perspectives, and it is your strategic responsibility to define what messages they will embrace and amplify, and the effect you want that to have on your future business strength.

12

Global Impact Underpins Greatest Value

Surely you'd rather be the one shaping your future than the one waiting to see what happens and then reacting. Today you have a unique opportunity to predict factors that are emerging and will affect your competitive success. I remember the emergence of the Internet, global communication networks, mobile telephony and even household computing. I remember being in the presence of those who captured the opportunities as well as those who demeaned its significance and failed to do so.

The future lies in connecting everything we do, everything we produce and consume, to the matter of its impact. Success can best be predicted by deciding how you can pre-emptively reshape the future competitive environment.

Your most significant difference will be how well your business affects things people care deeply about at a human level, globally. Looking across horizons, in time and across value chains, you can see that your impact could reach the whole of humanity in just a few links.

Soon you'll accept this isn't just a clever business idea, 'something Steve was excited about', but, rather, an obligation you have to secure the survival of your company and the betterment of global society. Do it well and you'll succeed and thrive. Do it poorly and you'll either fail terribly or survive unremarkably.

You could be the source of great leadership.
It's not about age, creds, or anything more
than a willingness to be that 'one'.

Face it – perhaps it is you the world is waiting for. You will doubt this if you're in a small company or acting alone. In fact, it's equally as relevant to you as to any business of any size, or to any politician or other influencer.

On the one hand, humans are at heart self-centred creatures who perhaps dream of self-determination, even immortality, until the moment it's proven otherwise at their deathbeds. Each person perceives a universe that encircles them in their own perception of reality. In a confusing contradiction, each of us doubts we can have any genuinely significant influence globally. We have evolved to exaggerate our importance, yet we have become brainwashed to accept dependence on a distant 'great leader' with the genius to show us the way.

By now, you will know my view. There's no such thing as the great leader of great genius who predetermines humanity's path. That is down to each individual and the combined effect of masses of individuals acting together, deciding a theme or movement that may then be expounded by some convenient spokesperson – enter, stage left, the 'leader'. Will you make your way to the stage preparing your speech, or wait in the audience for someone to step forward?

In Chapter 6 you read my story of the company we are referring to as ITCO, which embodies experiences I've had in real life. That was arguably a transformation in thought leadership of its time. I was lucky to have been attached to that, and I certainly benefitted from other great minds and experience above and around me in these businesses.

You'll recall my description of hostility faced when driving new business models, and how, in my mid-twenties, I was forced to become that chosen one. It wasn't a matter of age or experience because I lacked both. Yet, without doubt, great success was achieved because I was willing to step up and do the necessary, contradicting mainstream wisdom, being noncompliant with those in power. If I can be the one, surely anyone can.

Life-and-death impact can be one step away
from you, or ten steps – it doesn't matter.

I met a man who had in previous years been the Sudanese camp leader in Calais, France, where thousands had gathered seeking refuge in the UK. The public majority were, and perhaps still are, hostile towards asylum seekers. He and I became friends. With help from a few others this man's vision was brought to life.

A weekly group opened to support vulnerable asylum seekers. They visited together, talked, learned language and computer skills and found help where it wasn't otherwise available. I felt out of my depth, not able to contribute other than by showing my face occasionally. I was assured that this little was deeply valued.

I met another Sudanese man who'd been in a state of limbo for nine years. He was at risk of death if he returned to Sudan yet was denied asylum on a technicality. His elderly parents would possibly never see him again. I saw anger, hopelessness, fear and depression in a familiar mix that often sadly results in acts of self-harm.

I was the person present for him when he needed to vent these emotions. My role that day was simply to believe that I could make an impact – I was the one for that man at that moment. I connected him with a legal volunteer and three weeks later I was shocked by the transformation I saw when we met again. His case had been 'unlocked' and he was then on track for asylum. A life changed, perhaps even saved.

I cannot estimate how many people have been affected because we chose to support our friend in his dream to create this group. We can't foresee how many people will find roles in life that make a great impact on society, or children they will raise who might do the same.

If you take action to demonstrate your principles, you can expect there will be critics. You might get no awards and maybe even no rewards. If you believe it is the impact that counts, you must cast a pebble into the pond and accept you might never see the positive ripple effects directly. If you have faith that reward comes from having shown commitment to principles and values, then you will be less concerned about immediate return on investment.

I imagine that group saved more than one life, either directly or indirectly, but we will never know for sure. Choosing to act upon our principles, despite being met with disapproval by many, was a worthwhile choice. I know there are several people who observed this, and they now value me a little more for my principles. There were others who were indifferent, and some who were completely opposed.

You can't live life trying to impress everyone, only those who you choose for your target segment; who share similar principles and values; who will reward you with loyalty for being purpose-led in ways that are important to them at a human level.

I will never know the knock-on effect this had on my personal 'brand identity', but it almost certainly had one. There is no telling how far these values of tolerance and human collectiveness will cascade, but it is likely that they will do so to a greater or lesser extent. This is how, through the interconnected global human organism, we have an opportunity to influence others and ultimately to change the world.

The values that you attach to, and choose to champion, can and will cascade. These will travel through segments at a pace that other positive and negative influences have done before.

It is up to you to decide how to act upon that as an opportunity, or whether to wait until you observe this as an after-effect of other people's strategies. In the absence of a great divining leader laying a pathway for you, take a deep breath and go for it yourself. It's normal to care about the greater good, after satisfying self, family, tribe. Of course, they could all be interdependent.

Think about how important other people are to you at a human level, when compared with how much of your DNA they share.

Twins share 100% of their DNA. It's well known how bonded twins become in their commitment to one another. Parents and children share 50% of their DNA, as do siblings with each other. As a grandfather, uncle or half-sibling, I'll share 25% of my DNA with the other, with cousins 12.5%, and so it diminishes the further removed any relationship is.

Now consider, honestly, how your interest is affected by total disconnectedness from someone on the other side of the world who is from a different ethnicity and culture. It's not unusual if you feel more inclined to make decisions that are aligned with the interests of those sharing your DNA. You won't be likely to sacrifice the interests of family for the sake of people elsewhere in the world who you don't even know.

Such is the way of the world, and the instincts of humanity. I have no doubt this has served the interests of the survival of our species. Tribes of interdependent families have focused on what's good for them, thus co-creating, thriving and expanding.

We are at a point where foreign is equal to local, and global has the intimacy of home.

You may have heard the phrase, 'When America sneezes, the world catches a cold.' This perhaps explains why some British and European news channels report on US politics and economy more than that of neighbouring European countries.

That's accepted as a truism, because of the economic weight of the US, and the vulnerability of the global community due to its co-dependence with US economic wellbeing. We can see how the interests of a community totally remote from our own take on a significance normally reserved for domestic affairs in our own country.

Imagine a completely fictitious, hypothetical example: a condition being experienced in Romania that people in America care about with similar urgency. You might struggle to find an example, unless the Americans concerned with this are socially conscious about the supply chain consequences of consumerism on the lifestyle of young Romanians. Most Americans would struggle to show Romania on a map, let alone why they care.

Take a leap, perhaps only by a few years, and imagine another fictitious scenario: people see evidence that bad regulation of gold processing in Romania leaves traces of cyanide in gold used for American gold-plated jewellery, risking poisoning.

You probably know that the risk I describe is a practical impossibility. That doesn't matter, as it serves my need. In these circumstances, suddenly American families would urgently watch what's being done in Romania, demanding solutions to systemic corruption and better regulations for gold processing.

The dynamic of something affecting 'my family', or 'my tribe', no matter how remote that risk is, elevates its importance to a level equal to a domestic priority.

Today, a whole range of issues are accepted as being of urgent importance globally. I won't limit this to environmental issues, because they extend to all aspects of life. Themes include sustainability, resilience, ethical business practices and international development to create social and economic stability in all regions of the world. The idea of any country or company isolating completely is obviously both unwelcome and impractical. Thriving alone while ignoring ecosystem wellbeing, or a country ignoring international development, is short-termism at its worst.

Consumers and employees are becoming attuned to the impact that any business makes on these global issues. Customers won't necessarily be changing suppliers today on this basis, but soon it will become an imperative and soon a competitor will present that alternative that educates and satisfies the need.

Today they know that their family and tribe will soon somehow be affected, directly or indirectly. Perhaps this is not the case for all people. Statistically, it's less concerning for people of the baby boomer generation, nearing or in retirement. It most certainly is a priority for the consumers and workers of Gen Y (the Millennials) and Gen Z. It stands out as a priority of senior leaders from Gen X, who you can expect will be quick to embrace and act upon it.

Turning our attention to matters of global impact

This exposes profit-first, profit-last as being public enemy number one. I offer a hypothetical viewpoint for your consideration. You don't need to agree and that is your choice. I provide this now, because it is known to be a strongly held view among a large swathe of your customer base, whoever they might be. It is urgent that you understand.

The developed-world economies have changed a lot over the last few hundred years. If that is your home turf, then you probably don't live in tribal or village-centred systems like your forebears did. Back then people took care not to alienate neighbours, starve them or mess up the common environment. If you are under the belief that your present-day reality pervades globally, you are badly mistaken.

Welcome to the real world.

You don't need to look too far from home to see evidence that rural tribal and village-centred lifestyles remain the norm. Across humanity, those with artificially enhanced lifestyles in developed economies are the minority. That minority consumes and wastes a disproportionately high percentage of the whole, and in doing so that minority has created a system that abuses those less fortunate.

Most of humanity lives as our ancestors did, in situations ranging from nomadic or subsistence living, to lives of abject poverty and servitude.

If in doubt, consider this: World Bank data reported in 2018 showed that 26.2% of the world's population were living on less than $3.20 per day in 2015. Close to 46% of the world's population was living on less than $5.50 a day.[43]

For a few generations the developed nations have pillaged the world, first as colonial powers, then as industrial powers. Military interventions were presented back to us as being 'to protect the interests of freedom and economy'. While it did serve that

---

43   World Bank, 'Nearly half the world lives on less than $5.50 a day'

aim, the bigger picture was nothing short of enslavement of the underdeveloped world, for the profit of a few wealthy industrialists.

Those of us who live in developed economies felt complicit. We benefitted through lifestyles being modestly more comfortable than less fortunate billions living elsewhere. While we appear free, we seemingly exist here only to consume – inexorably, it seems. The satisfaction of our material demand has two purposes, and those are the creation of profit and sustaining conditions in which we consume more.

I feel compelled to ask whether this is all we can amount to as a species, as if we were created to perpetuate consumption with disregard for our world and the rest of humanity. I refuse to accept this, as we are greater than that, better in so many ways.

Problems 'over there' can't be ignored –
solve at point of origin in your business.

We can no longer excuse our responsibility to solve issues because of 'respect for the sovereignty of other nations'. We do this as a matter of course. You may have seen documentaries about 1950s nuclear weapons testing in the South Pacific islands. Inhabitants still struggle to force foreign governments to compensate properly for the harm caused there. It's an old habit that we struggle to shake off. Today this is reoccurring through irresponsible global outsourcing of waste processing that remains at unprecedented levels.

In 2018 nearly 160,000 containers filled with plastic waste were sent from the US to other countries where poor waste management regulations resulted in those plastics polluting the oceans. Over and over, we hear 'sovereignty of nations' being used as a convenient excuse when it suits, devolving liability for that crisis to poor countries.

An educated population of consumers will see through these excuses, although perhaps not immediately or by their own initiative. Despite this information being available, consumers still fail to penalise industries that are addicted to plastic packaging. A moment will come soon when by osmosis consumers will evolve a greater activism embodied by changing demand patterns. Savvy suppliers will solve this issue at point of origin, forming a differentiation that has the potential to sink their competitors. Governments and regulators must complete the cycle as the third part of the virtuous triangle.

I know of a materials technology innovation that is entering the market right now. Their compound fully and safely biodegrades fugitive plastics, leaving no microplastics behind. Boutique products have started respecifying packaging to leverage this compound as a differentiator in their markets. It is an example of how a major product provider acting upon this for all its packaging will re-educate consumers. Popular demand may then drive industry-wide change.

I'm guessing, at time of writing, that you maybe didn't know about this. You can see that unforeseeable innovations by competitors can cause disruptions you don't anticipate. Many of these issues are urgent to a whole generation of consumers. You and your people could be uniquely able to visualise a similar cause and effect you could influence. If so, this is where a near-and-present opportunity or threat exists.

Here's some free advice – if you package your products, you could use such an innovative compound to differentiate and build brand value. Test that and you'll probably find you'll gain loyalty from consumers that match themselves with these principles. Or you can wait, and one day pretend to be surprised when a competitor succeeds.

The three parts of the virtuous triangle – government and regulators, businesses, and customers – will always, inevitably, move with the pressures they receive from adjacent forces. It may be true that the big issues can only be finally resolved by singular massive steps taken globally by governments or the largest companies, but those steps will only ever take place because of many smaller steps taken around the world in the context of many business ecosystems.

The new normal mindset is one of a generation waiting for an alternative they can support.

While this might sound like anticapitalist extremism, I assure you it is not. I am an ethical responsible capitalist, not a socialist. We are quickly moving from a focus on pure growth to a new priority of being resilient as a species. We are moving from a time of profit-first, profit-last towards prevalence of stakeholder capitalism. This is a threat to businesspeople who don't yet embrace this changing reality, and it is an opportunity for those who do. That is why I've written this book to help you navigate and succeed in that Great Shift.

This is how billions of people are thinking today. It is not revolutionary thinking. To entire generations of people, this way of thinking is now already their new normal. It is a self-perpetuating social movement that is already a Great Shift. You just might not have noticed yet.

How, then, can anyone be remotely surprised that the profit-first, profit-last era is nearing its end, quickly? My sons' generation are acutely aware of the global injustice we preside over. That is worsening because this system seems hellbent on perpetuating its profit regardless of the cost to humanity and our environment.

The UN Secretary-General spoke out about the climate emergency and challenged governments and businesses for lying, adding fuel to the flames by turning a blind eye to their undertakings, and effectively accelerating us towards disaster. Consumers, it seems, are addicted to wasteful consumption. Businesses are addicted to growth and profit. Governments are addicted to perpetuating their systems.[44]

Do we imagine this can continue indefinitely? All evidence shows us that is impossible. Imagine the time when markets apportion blame to the guilty and rewards to those who attempted to help. Which will you be?

That there are voices who demean the determination of this generation, or its willingness to inconvenience itself in the interests of others, is a moot point. It is no longer a question of whether enough demand and energy exist for change to occur.

The real question is whether there are options available that allow people to vent that demand and satisfy their hunger for change.

---

44   UN Secretary-General, 'Secretary-General warns of climate emergency'

The only test that matters is *not* whether a generation will stop consuming certain products because of a brand's corporate malfeasance or the brand's ignorance of global issues that matter most. It is whether, or I should say when, alternatives arise that transform sectors based on purpose-led and principles-focused differentiation. Take that same point and extrapolate it to every competitive market, and the same can be said to be true.

Knowing your global impact is no longer optional –
the Great Shift is real.

Ask whether you understand your global impact. You may see that your impact is becoming the only buying criteria of consequence. If you don't know what your impact is, whether it's positive or negative, then you have serious questions to answer. Not least of which is how you can possibly remain attractive or competitive in comparison to those who are clear about this.

The beliefs and choices of aging Gen Y and Gen Z will change the face of how you compete for employees and customers. Generations and global economic evolution will affect demand and supply. Online research tells me 70% of Gen X and 54% of Millennials and Gen Z are likely to stop shopping at a company that supports a practice or issue that they disagree with. Among baby boomers, only 37% would do the same.[45]

Overlay onto this a shift towards supply-side power in many emerging economies. Having survived conditions imposed on

---

45　Cox, 'How corporate social responsibility influences buying decisions' them by developed industrial countries, new forms of impact will be exerted. This is caused by shared experiences among billions in maturing generations of consumers and employees, with increasing spending budgets and freedom to select employment, who until now have existed simply to serve the few in developed nations.

When you consider the aging and evolving socioeconomic patterns I've referred to, you see it's inevitable that businesses now need to think carefully about what they stand for and put that into action. If you don't, your competitors will.

Up to the point of this generational transition, the compliant nature of consumers and employees guided consumption and employment choices. We were conditioned to accept norms offered to us, and to buy products just the way they were supplied.

Industry was led by older generations, competition was relatively low and innovation costly, so disruptions were time-consuming to achieve. Alternative choices were fewer than we'd have liked to demand and so power was in the hands of the producers. Their decision criteria were almost exclusively profit-focused. With those elders having no incentive to change, younger generations had no power to force it.

We are moving into a time when younger generations feel motivated and empowered, so their demand dictates supply.

This new demand will be fulfilled by easier, lower cost and more accessible capability to innovate. Disruption supply-side will be helped by an emerging surge of demand there, and by sources of innovative capabilities fed from emerging economies experiencing rapid development and generation shift. Differentiated offerings solving critical global priorities will emerge from new entrants, or perhaps from incumbents with the vision to embrace change.

Act today to secure future success

Way back in Chapters 2, 4 and 5, there is a description of what I called the virtuous triangle of consumers and employees, governments and regulators, and businesses. Throughout this book, I've emphasised the symbiosis in ecosystems; ideas taking root become prevailing opinions in populations; and later, leaders rising to dominance based on strategies that reflect their agility to grasp and adapt prevailing opinions.

You can predict that a great generational change in opinions, demand and choices will gather until a critical mass is achieved to cause a tipping point, creating a new norm. That will influence steps taken by governments and regulators and will also dictate which businesses and people will arise as the new leaders.

The tipping point is there to be seen.
Act upon it professionally.

Values that emerge as priority, and empowerment both in consumers and supply-side, is changing the landscape across our globalised interconnected human organism. You have read how the 200 million businesses and businesspeople operating there are the most effective vehicle to seek out and deliver beneficial changes.

Laws will change soon enough, but that is not what you should sit and wait for. Glory goes to the brave of heart. If you accept the main thesis I present here, you will know that the biggest prizes go to those who think ahead and act upon it.

Conclusion

You don't need to look far to find the sources of ideas. Listening to your own people and business ecosystem with genuine curiosity will help you uncover the ideas and changes that are desired most urgently by consumers and employees, and the principles that will result in loyalty. Embrace the nonconformists and contrarians, because they're the ones who will take you in unforeseen directions. At the same time keep a firm grip so you can bring back focus onto getting the job done.

Align yourself with global issues that matter to most people deeply at a human level, regardless of the scale of impact. This will be likely to resonate immediately and could become a vital differentiator both now and in the future.

Learn to use frameworks, methods, tools and techniques, professionally and wisely. Get some help and learn to be better at using the insights gained. That will directly improve financial performance and will result in increased company-level valuation.

Being inclusive of people in your team and across your ecosystem will create a force of evangelists that will spread news of your purpose-led differentiation. Encourage respectful challenge to make sure your choices are right and that you are reactive to changing dynamics that your people will discover before you can.

Tuning into all sources of positive and negative energy, study forms of influence between these people, and through those channels you will activate strategy to greatest possible effect.

Your deadline is now.

This is likely to become one of the greatest causes of discontinuity in businesses that we've ever seen. Conversely, this is also a key enabler for future success in business. It will be difficult to remain relevant unless businesspeople can clearly state what they stand for. This could be in terms of values and principles-led strategy, or simply what impact is being made in the interconnected value chains of one's ecosystem – both positive impact and resolving previous negative effects.

We have grown accustomed to disruptive innovations that are sector-specific, leading to sector-specific extinction events. Typically, these have been noticeable as aspects of our value chain, which allows us time to decide precisely when and how to act on it. You have read how to plan for evolving scenarios across time horizons and in your ecosystem's interconnected value chains. That will help you to make a decision on how and when to act based on the emergence of unforeseen wide-ranging events as they unfold, using scenario planning and monitoring changes as they occur.

This Great Shift will be a pan-sector disruption event second to none. It is simmering away in the background of your competitive landscape. Employees and customers are just waiting for viable alternatives to arise. As soon as alternatives appear that better serve a burgeoning and overwhelming desire for satisfaction, the dial on employment and buying choices will move without warning.

Whether this is perceived as an opportunity or a threat by you will largely be determined by how you react, by the course of action you decide and whether you act now or opt to wait and see. I sincerely hope you make the right choices.

Good luck. Stay in touch to let me know how you get along. Do ask for help.

Bibliography

Anwar, M, *Love as a Business Strategy: Resilience, belonging and success* (Lioncrest, 2021)

Brower, T, 'The power of purpose and why it matters now', *Forbes* (22 August 2021), www.forbes.com/sites/tracybrower/2021/08/22/the-power-of-purpose-and-why-it-matters-now, accessed 22 March 2022

Carnegie, D, *How to Win Friends and Influence People* (Simon & Schuster, 2006)

Christensen, CM, *The Innovator's Dilemma: When new technologies cause great firms to fail* (Harvard Business School Press, 1997; reprint edn, 2013)

Clark, D, 'Estimated number of companies worldwide from 2000 to 2020' (Statista, 3 September 2021), www.statista.com/statistics/1260686/global-companies, accessed 16 March 2022

Cole, NL, 'What is cultural hegemony?' *ThoughtCo.* (5 January 2020), www.thoughtco.com/cultural-hegemony-3026121, accessed 15 January 2022

'Contrarian', definition in *The Free Dictionary* (no date), www.thefreedictionary.com/contrarian, accessed 1 February 2022

Covey, SR, *The 7 Habits of Highly Effective People* (Simon & Schuster, 1999)

Cox, TA, 'How corporate social responsibility influences buying decisions' (Clutch, 1969), https://clutch.co/pr-firms/resources/how-corporate-social-responsibility-influences-buying-decisions, accessed 16 March 2022

Democracy Now, 'School strike for climate: meet 15-year-old activist Greta Thunberg, who inspired a global movement' [video] (11 December 2018), www.democracynow.org/2018/12/11/meet_the_15_year_old_swedish, accessed 1 February 2022

Dongoski, R, 'Plant-based protein predictions: When might the term "alternative protein" be obsolete?' (EY, 2021), https://ey.com/en_us/agribusiness/when-might-the-term-alternative-protein-be-obsolete, accessed 16 March 2022

Emmer, M, '95 percent of new products fail. Here are 6 steps to make sure yours don't', *Inc.* (6 July 2018), www.inc.com/marc-emmer/95-percent-of-new-products-fail-here-are-6-steps-to-make-sure-yours-dont.html, accessed 17 March 2022

en-academic, 'The Thirty-Six Stratagems' (Wikimedia Foundation, 2010), https://en-academic.com/dic.nsf/enwiki/358214, accessed 15 January 2022

EPIC: The Embankment Project for Inclusive Capitalism (Coalition for Inclusive Capitalism, 2018), www.coalitionforinclusivecapitalism.com/epic, accessed 19 April 2022

Fairtrade Foundation, 'Half of global consumers used their buying power to make a positive difference during the pandemic' (7 July 2021), www.fairtrade.org.uk/media-centre/news/half-of-global-consumers-used-their-buying-power-to-make-a-positive-difference-during-the-pandemic, accessed 16 March 2022

Frankl, VE, *Yes to Life – in spite of everything* (Penguin Random House, 2020)

Gibbins-Klein, M, *The Thoughtful Leader* (Panoma Press, 2015)

Gibbins-Klein, M, 'Thought leadership – thoughtful leadership', https://mindygk.com, accessed 25 March 2022

Gladwell, M, *Blink: The power of thinking without thinking* (Penguin, 2006)

Hambrick, D, and Fredrickson, J, 'Are you sure you have a strategy?', *Academy of Management Executive*, 15/4 (2001)

Hutton, G, and Ward, M, *Business Statistics* (House of Commons Library, 2021), https://researchbriefings.files.parliament.uk/documents/SN06152/SN06152.pdf, accessed 16 March 2022

Institute for Strategy and Competitiveness, 'The Value Chain' (Harvard Business School, no date), www.isc.hbs.edu/strategy/business-strategy/Pages/the-value-chain.aspx, accessed 16 March 2022

Institute of Directors, www.iod.com, accessed 25 March 2022

Jones, S, and Knotts, TL, 'Factors affecting innovator success and failure', presented at US Patent and Trademark Office National Inventors Conference,

January 2002, www.researchgate.net/publication/320106963_Factors_
Affecting_Innovator_Success_and_Failure, accessed 19 April 2022

Keller, V, *The Business Case For Purpose* (Harvard Business Review,
1 October 2015), https://hbr.org/sponsored/2015/10/the-business-case-for-
purpose, accessed 1 February 2022

Mannheim, K, 'The problem of generations'. In P. Kecskemeti (ed), *Essays on
the Sociology of Knowledge* (Routledge and Kegan Paul, 1952), pp276–320

Marks, JW, 'Medical definition of Hippocratic oath' (MedicineNet,
2021), www.medicinenet.com/hippocratic_oath/definition.htm, accessed
22 March 2022

Marks, RJ, 'Einstein's only rejected paper', *Mind Matters* (14 May 2020),
https://mindmatters.ai/2020/05/einsteins-only-rejected-paper, accessed
1 February 2022

Maslow, AH, 'A theory of human motivation', *Psychological Review*, 50/4 (1943),
pp370–396, https://doi.org/10.1037/h0054346, accessed 16 March 2022

MIRECC, 'Unit size (US Army in the late 20th century)' (US Department of
Veterans Affairs, no date), www.mirecc.va.gov/docs/visn6/8_US_Military_
Unit_Size.pdf, accessed 1 February 2022

National Academies of Sciences, Engineering, Medicine, *Are Generational
Categories Meaningful Distinctions For Workforce Management?* (National Academies,
2020), https://nap.nationalacademies.org/catalog/25796/are-generational-
categories-meaningful-distinctions-for-workforce-management, accessed
7 April 2022

National Statistics Institute, 'Spain number of companies: 1998–2020' (CEIC,
2020), www.ceicdata.com/en/spain/number-of-companies-by-region/no-of-
companies, accessed 16 March 2022

North American Industry Classification System, 'Custom counts' (NAICS
Association, 2021), www.naics.com/business-lists/counts-by-company-size,
accessed 16 March 2022

Organisation for Economic Co-operation and Development, 'Who are the
owners of the world's listed companies and why should we care?' (OECD,

17 October 2019), www.oecd.org/corporate/who-are-the-owners-of-the-worlds-listed-companies-and-why-should-we-care.htm, accessed 16 March 2022

Peters, T, 'Excellence now!', https://tompeters.com, accessed 16 March 2022

Peters, T, Waterman Jr, RH, and Waterman, RH, *In Search of Excellence* (Harper & Row, 1982)

Phillips, S, 'The change man', www.simonphillipstcm.com, accessed 16 March 2022

Porter, ME, 'How competitive forces shape strategy', *Harvard Business Review* (March–April 1979), https://hbr.org/1979/03/how-competitive-forces-shape-strategy, accessed 16 March 2022

Porter, ME, *On Competition* (Harvard Business Review Press, 2008)

Porter, ME, *The Competitive Advantage: Creating and sustaining superior performance* (Free Press, 1985)

Power, P, et al, *Success Secrets of Entrepreneurs* (Panoma Press, 2022)

Quote Investigator, 'The Secret of change…' (28 May 2013), https://quoteinvestigator.com/2013/05/28/socrates-energy, accessed 1 Feb 2022

Rosnow, RL, and Foster, EK, 'Rumor and gossip research', *American Psychological Association* (April 2005), www.apa.org/science/about/psa/2005/04/gossip, accessed 16 March 2022,

Sanders, S, 'Five Horizons Model', www.fivehorizonsmodel.com

Sustainable Development Goals, 'Gross National Happiness Index' (United Nations, no date), https://sustainabledevelopment.un.org/index.php?page=view&type=99&nr=266&menu=1449, accessed 16 March 2022

Sustainable Development Goals, '17 goals to transform our world' (United Nations, no date), www.un.org/sustainabledevelopment, accessed 16 March 2022

Tolstoy, L, *War and Peace* (Penguin, 2007)

Travers, J, and Milgram, S, 'An experimental study of the small world problem', *Sociometry*, 32 (1969), pp425–443, https://psycnet.apa.org/doi/10.2307/2786545, accessed 16 March 2022

UNaLAB, 'Walt Disney method' (no date), https://unalab.enoll.org/walt-disney-method, accessed 7 April 2022

University of British Columbia, '2021 honorary degree recipients' (no date), https://graduation.ok.ubc.ca/event/honorary-degrees/2021-honorary-degree-recipients, accessed 1 February 2022

UN Secretary-General, 'Secretary-General warns of climate emergency, calling intergovernmental panel's report "a file of shame", while saying leaders "are lying", fuelling flames' (UN, 4 April 2022), www.un.org/press/en/2022/sgsm21228.doc.htm, accessed 7 April 2022

UppyBags, 'About us' (no date), https://uppybags.com/pages/about-recycle-material-bag-brand, accessed 16 March 2022

Warwick Business School, www.wbs.ac.uk, accessed 18 March 2022

World Bank, 'Nearly half the world lives on less than $5.50 a day' (17 October 2018), www.worldbank.org/en/news/press-release/2018/10/17/nearly-half-the-world-lives-on-less-than-550-a-day, accessed 2 February 2022

Acknowledgements

I'd like to thank the following people, who were instrumental in supporting me during the writing of this book.

For invaluable guidance and feedback on refining the manuscript, Tony Cooper, Lisa Burton, Stephen Chadwick, Michael Butler, Joe Bridgeman and Steve Hanney.

Mindy Gibbins-Klein, my book coach and founder of The Book Midwife, for being a source of great discipline and experience which enabled me to write this book.

My dear late father, Peter, who applied the phrase 'just do it' long before the shoe brand trademarked it, and who believed in me before anyone else.

My sons Devon, Jadon and Brandon, who lived alongside me through the years when I experienced many of the events depicted in this book – they shared a tough reality with maturity and graciousness, and for them I have only love and admiration.

My dear Svetlana, who picked up where my father left off, strengthening my self-belief and resolve to create a better future, and frequently visiting me in my parallel universe of authoring, bearing gifts of kindness, food and liquid with a smile.

The Author

Steve is a go-to-market strategist, boosting company-level value, rethinking ambitions and then embedding systematic enablers for scale success. That equips companies to pivot, or course-correct, in initiatives affecting product-to-service shift, go-to-market acceleration, pursuits, routes-to-market partnerships and continual improvement of readiness.

Having built businesses and rescued businesses to multibillions of dollars, Steve's approach and models are embraced in start-ups, scale-ups and corporates. This includes Five Horizons, Proposition Transformation, Business Growth Mechanics and more. Challenging norms has become a helpful habit. As a respectful nonconformist, Steve deconstructs assumptions limiting potential, reforming for success.

Challenge enriches life. A father of three young men, he continues to learn from them. Despite a lifelong fear of deep water, he's often seen out on sea kayaks. A fellow of the Institute of Directors, and MBA strategy guest speaker at WBS, Steve co-authored *Success Secrets of Entrepreneurs*, and is board advisor supporting several open-minded entrepreneurs and senior executives.

🌐 https://linktr.ee/stevesanders